INSTRUCTOR'S RESOURCE BOOK F(
Microeconomics
Second Edition

INSTRUCTOR'S RESOURCE BOOK FOR

Microeconomics

Second Edition

B. Curtis Eaton
Simon Fraser University

Diane F. Eaton

W. H. Freeman and Company
New York

Copyright © 1991 by B. Curtis Eaton and Diane F. Eaton

Classroom Experiments © 1991 by W. H. Freeman and Compan

No part of this book may be reproduced by any mechanical, photographic, or electronic process, or in the form of a phonographic recording, nor may it be stored in a retrieval system, transmitted, or otherwise copied for public or private use, without written permission from the publisher.

ISBN 0-7167-2183-X

Printed in the United States of America

1 2 3 4 5 6 7 8 9 0   LH   9 9 8 7 6 5 4 3 2 1

Contents

Solutions — 1

Chapter 1	1
Chapter 2	1
Chapter 3	3
Chapter 4	4
Chapter 5	8
Chapter 6	14
Chapter 7	18
Chapter 8	20
Chapter 9	23
Chapter 10	25
Chapter 11	27
Chapter 12	30
Chapter 13	32
Chapter 14	32
Chapter 15	35
Chapter 16	36
Chapter 17	37

Classroom Experiments — 41

Experiment 1	42
Experiment 2	45
Experiment 3	47
Experiment 4	53
Experiment 5	55
Experiment 6	58
Experiment 7	60
Experiment 8	65
Experiment 9	69
Experiment 10	75

Transparency Masters — 81

Solutions

CHAPTER 1

1.1 As the Hotelling model illustrates, equilibrium and optimality are quite separate concepts. The equilibrium of the Hotelling model is not Pareto optimal, nor is it cost-benefit optimal.

1.2 Let a, b, and c denote the three locations and assume that a < b < c. Equilibrium requires that a be just less than b, and that c be just greater than b. But the middle firm is then not in equilibrium since it could increase its profit by moving just to the left of a or to the right of c.

1.3 In both versions of the model, any pair of locations is Pareto optimal. Consider any configuration of the two firms. Try to find another configuration in which at least one party is better off and none are worse off. It can't be done, and hence the initial configuration is Pareto optimal.

1.4 With no loss of generality we can restrict All-Valu's location to the interval from 0 to 1/2. Let a denote All-Valu's location. For any location a in this interval, Bestway will choose to locate just to the right of a, All-Valu's market segment will extend from 0 to a, and its profit will be (P - C)Na. Since its profit increases as a increases, All-Valu will choose location 1/2.

1.5 Both firms will locate at 12 o'clock.

CHAPTER 2

2.1 In the initial situation, equilibrium price is 13 and equilibrium quantity is 7. Subsequently, equilibrium price rises to 17 and equilibrium quantity rises to 11.

2.2 The restriction in supply means that the supply curve for drugs will shift up and to the left, resulting in an increase in equilibrium price and a decrease in equilibrium quantity. One would anticipate an increase (a decrease) in street crime if the amount drug users spend on drugs is larger (smaller) in the subsequent equilibrium than in the initial equilibrium.

2.3 Time spent in lineups for goods played a large role in the allocation of goods in the Soviet Union. That is, time prices perform the allocative function if money prices are fixed. In addition, a variety of corrupt practices emerged to solve the allocation problem in the Soviet Union.

2.4 The voluntary export restrictions shift the supply of Japanese cars up and to the left, resulting in a decrease in equilibrium quantity and an increase in equilibrium price of Japanese cars. This price increase in turn shifts the demand for American cars up and to the right, since Japanese cars are substitutes for American cars. This demand shift will increase both the equilibrium price and the equilibrium quantity of American cars.

2.5 The function of parking meters is to allocate scarce parking spaces, not to make a profit. In retailing districts, for example, one purpose of parking meters is to induce retail employees to park in less convenient spots so that customers of the retail stores can find convenient parking. In the absence of parking meters, fewer customers would visit the retail district, generating less retail business and fewer jobs.

2.6 The amount of trash left by the roadside will be larger in the fee for service regime, and the amount hauled to the dump will be larger in the case where there is no fee for service. There in now considerable evidence that the total amount of refuse is significantly smaller under the fee for service arrangement.

2.7 a) Newspapers would be induced to economize on the amount of paper they used. Hence, one would expect smaller papers and tighter formats. The price of advertising space in newspapers would increase, inducing advertisers to substitute away from newspapers and toward magazines, radio, and T. V.

b) All users of paper would be induced to economize on their use of paper. Hence, less paper would be produced and there would be lees paper to dispose of. However, one would expect users of paper to substitute other materials, plastic for instance, for paper. The disposal problems associated with these materials would be exacerbated by the tax on paper.

c) There are many possibilities here. For example, paper manufacturers could be required to use a specified portion of recycled fiber in the manufacture of paper products, which would create a demand for used paper, thereby creating private economic incentives to recycle paper. The key to any successful scheme is to somehow create a demand for used paper.

CHAPTER 3

3.1 These two curves intersect and hence could not be two indifference curves for the same person.

3.2 Dizzy's indifference curves are vertical lines. The following are utility functions for Dizzy: x_1, $10x_1$, $\log x_1$, $x_1 - 77$. Indeed, any monotonically increasing function of x_1 will represent Dizzy's preferences.

3.3 a) Letting good 1 be $20 bills and good 2 be $5 bills, the following is an indifference curve: $200 = 10x_1 + 40x_2$. MRS of $20 bills for $5 bills is 1/4.

b) If the consumer has two feet, the indifference curves will have right angled kinks along the line $x_2 = x_1$. Above the kink, they will be vertical, and to the right of the kink they will be horizontal. If the consumer has only one foot then indifference curves will be vertical or horizontal depending on which foot the consumer has.

c) The indifference curve will be concave to the origin, and downward sloping.

d) Letting x_1 represent quantity of lobster and x_2 represent money, the indifference curve will be u-shaped. In the upward sloping portion, if the individual is forced to eat more lobster, more money is required to get him or her back to the indifference curve. With free disposal, the upward sloping portion of the indifference curve is replaced by a horizontal line.

e) The indifference curve be a straight line with slope equal to -1.

f) The indifference curve will be upward sloping.

3.4 a) All three indifference curves are coincident.

b) The second utility function can be derived from the first by multiplying by 10, and the third can be derived from the first by squaring. Hence all three functions represent the same preference ordering.

3.5 a) Her indifference curves have right angled kinks along the line $2x_1 = 7x_2$, and are vertical above the kink and horizontal to the right of it.

b) Her preferences satisfy neither the nonsatiation nor the smoothness assumption. Her indifference curves are only weakly convex.

c) More of one good does not always make Althea better off. If, for example, $2x_1 > 7x_2$, then increasing x_1 does not make her better off.

3.6 First plot the indifference curve for utility number 36. To get the indifference curve for utility number 49 (64) move the first one vertically up by 13 (28) units. Hence, along any vertical line all three indifference curves have the same slope.

3.7 The indifference curves from the previous problem meet these conditions.

3.8 a) This indifference curve is composed of two segments: the line $x_2 = 10$, for $x_1 < 10$; the line $x_1 = 10$, for $x_2 < 10$. The two segments intersect at (10, 10).

b) $U(x_1, x_2) = \max(x_1, x_2)$, where max means the maximum of.

c) Jack's preferences do not satisfy the nonsatiation, smoothness, and convexity assumptions.

3.9 Jo's indifference curves are vertical lines for $x_1 \leq 3$, and for bundles with more than 3 units of x_1 they are convex. (It may be useful to think of them as convex to an origin at (3, 0).) Moving from left to right along any horizontal line with $x_2 > 0$, we encounter more preferred indifference curves.

CHAPTER 4

4.1 First draw the Engel curve, and suppose the good is good 1. Notice that good 1 is normal for low levels of income and inferior for high levels of income. Hence the income-consumption path will have the shape of a backward C: it will initially have a positive slope and subsequently a negative slope. The slope of any indifference curve will be $-p_1/p_2$ where the indifference curve intersects the income-consumption path.

4.2 MRS is identical and equal to $-p_1/p_2$ at these two bundles, assuming that indifference curves are smooth.

4.3 a) Rita certainly will be no worse off since she can buy bundle (100, 50) after p_1 and her income increase. If her indifference curves are smooth, she will be better off.

b) It is now uncertain what happens to Rita's well being. She may be better off, worse off, or just as well off.

4.4 Since good 1 is not a Giffen good, p_1 must be larger at bundle (10, 23) than at bundle (15, 40). Hence, MRS must be larger at (10, 23) than at (15, 40).

4.5 We know the following and nothing more: one of the goods is inferior and the other is normal.

4.6 Each of Jack's indifference curves intersects the x_2 axis but not the x_1 axis. Hence, good 1 is inessential and good 2 is essential.

4.7 The demand for wheat appears to be inelastic with respect to price.

4.8 a) Ted's demand functions are $x_1 = .4M/p_1$, and $x_2 = .6M/p_2$.

b) The income consumption path is the line $x_2 = 3x_1/2$. The Engel curves are $x_1 = .4M$ and $x_2 = .6M$.

4.9 In this case quantity demanded of good 1 is independent of income, and hence the income elasticity of demand for good 1 is 0.

4.10 These results are easily shown using the graphic trick for computing price elasticity that we developed in our discussion of Figure 4.16.

4.11 a) Because the price consumption path is horizontal, we see that Nancy's expenditure on good 2 does not change as p_1 changes. Hence, her expenditure on good 1 does not change as p_1 changes.

b) Let the portion of income spent on good 1 in this exercise be z. Then, her demand for good 1, given p_2, is $x_1 = zM/p_1$.

c) Good 2 is neither a substitute nor a complement for good 1.

d) Price elasticity of demand for good 1 is 1.

4.12 Suppose the individual's income is $1000, and the price of medical services is $1 per unit, and imagine that the individual currently consumes 100 units of medical services. If price rose to $10, the individual would need all his or her income to buy 100 units. Hence, in this illustration, it's impossible for demand to be perfectly price inelastic for prices in excess of $10.

4.13 a) As p_1 increases we move from left to right along the price-consumption path. As we do so, expenditure on good 2 increases; hence expenditure on good 1 decreases, indicating that the demand for good 1 is inelastic with respect to the price of good 1.

b) As p_1 increases demand for good 2 increases, indicating that good 1 is a substitute for good 2.

4.14 We can solve the following simultaneous equations to get Brett's demand functions.

$$p_1/p_2 = x_2/x_1$$
$$p_1 x_1 + p_2 x_2 = M$$

They are $x_1 = M/(2p_1)$ and $x_2 = M/(2p_2)$. Both goods are normal since quantity demanded increases as income increases. For both goods price and quantity demanded are inversely related, hence neither is a Giffen good. Since quantity demanded is positive no matter how high the good's price rises, both goods are essential.

4.15 Since the income-consumption path is positively sloped, both goods are normal. Neither good is a Giffen good since Giffen goods are necessarily inferior.

4.16 The budget line is composed of two segments. Suppose that electricity is good 1. For $x_1 < 10$, the slope of the budget line is -1, and for $x_1 > 10$, the slope is -3/2. Utility maximizing solutions on the two segments of the budget line, and at the kink in the budget line, are possible. Assuming that indifference curves are smooth and convex, if MRS at the kink is less than 1, then the solution will be on the flat portion of the budget line. If MRS at the kink is greater than 3/2, then the solution will be on the steep portion of the budget line. If MRS at the kink is greater than 1 and less than 3/2, then the solution will be at the kink.

4.17 Mr. Lucky's budget line is $1.25x_1 + x_2 = 1250$. The opportunity cost of $1 spent today is $1.25 that cannot be spent tomorrow.

4.18 Not-So's budget line is identical to Mr. Lucky'y.

4.19 Consider a good like gas for your car. When the price of gas is very low, you might buy and drive a real gas-guzzler. Now if the price of gas increases a great deal, you can economize in the short term by driving your gas-guzzler less often and at slower speeds, while in the long term you have the added option of buying a more fuel efficient car. Thus in cases where it easier to change consumption habits in the long term than in the short term, demand tends to more elastic with respect to price in the long term.

4.20 Figure 4.20 is useful here. Good 1 is candy bars and good 2 is a composite commodity. The initial equilibrium is at E, and the final equilibrium is at D. The increase in the child's allowance is distance AD, and the tax collected on the sale of candy bars is distance AC, which is less than AD. And the child consumes fewer candy bars in the subsequent equilibrium. So long as the child's indifference curves are smooth and convex, these results are generally true.

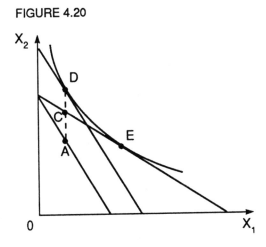

FIGURE 4.20

4.21 Figure 4.21 is useful here. The worst point on the budget line is the point of tangency at F. The utility maximizing bundle is at E, where quantity demanded of good 1 is 0, and all income is spent on good 2. If the budget line was flatter, the utility maximizing bundle would include 0 units of good 2 and all income would be spent on good 1.

FIGURE 4.21

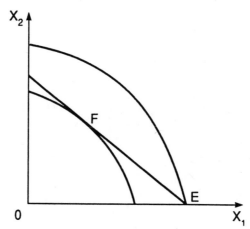

4.22 Consider some bundle A on the budget line, and suppose that the indifference curve through bundle A is locally concave. Then, if the budget line is steeper than the indifference curve at point A, bundles on the budget line immediately to the left of A are preferred to bundle A. If the budget line is flatter than the indifference curve at point A, bundles on the budget line immediately to the right of A are preferred to bundle A. If the budget line is tangent to the indifference curve, then bundles immediately to the right and left of A are preferred to A.

CHAPTER 5

5.1 If Joe's indifference curves are smooth and convex, he will prefer the lump-sum tax, and he will smoke more cigarettes with that tax than with the sales tax. If his indifference curves are kinked, then it is possible that he would be indifferent to the two taxes; if he is indifferent, then he would consume the same number of cigarettes under both taxes.

5.2 Figures 5.2a and 5.2b are useful here. In 5.2a, indifference curves are smooth and convex and the individual strictly prefers the lump-sum subsidy. In 5.2b, indifference curves are kinked and the individual is indifferent to the two subsidy schemes.

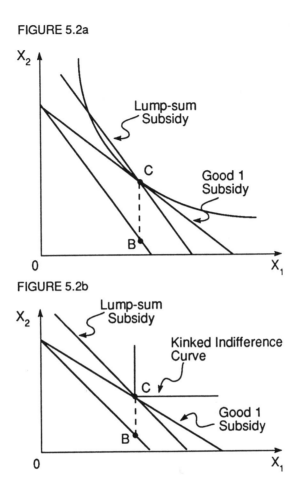

FIGURE 5.2a

FIGURE 5.2b

5.3 Think of the students as forming a coffee club, and review in-chapter Problem 5.2. Assuming that the representative student's indifference curves are smooth and convex, the reasoning outlined in that problem reveals that the representative student will be better off with the $10 loan and coffee at $.25 per cup than he or she would be with Jane selling coffee at $.75 per cup until she recovers her $490.

5.4 Figures 5.4a and 5.4b are useful here. The crucial price differential is (a) distance EF in Figure 5.4a, and (b) it is the cross-hatched area in Figure 5.4b, assuming that Buff's demand for instant photographs is independent of her income.

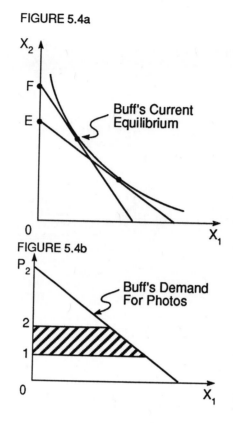

FIGURE 5.4a

FIGURE 5.4b

5.5 a) $5000, b) $3600, c) $1300

5.6 To maximize profit, Walt should sell weekly passes for $50, and charge nothing for each ride. His profit will be $5000 per week, and each kid will take 10 rides per week.

5.7 a) The budget line is illustrated in Figure 5.7, on the following page.

b) Yes, assuming that indifference curves are smooth and convex.

c) This indifference curve in Figure 5.7 illustrates this case.

5.8 Figure 5.8 is useful. The initial equilibrium is at A, and the subsequent equilibrium at B. Since Ralph works more than 40 hours in the initial equilibrium, the wage increase for his primary job, where he can work just 40 hours, involves only an income effect. Hence, since leisure is a normal good, Ralph works less at B than at A.

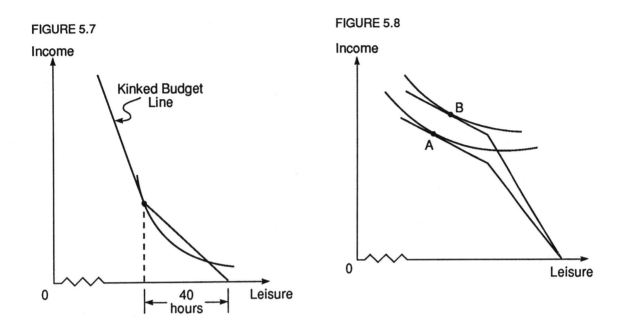

5.9 Assuming that her indifference curves are smooth and convex, she would choose the 20% increase in her wage rate. See Figure 5.9.

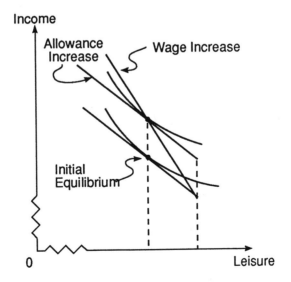

5.10 If more seats were made available, more students would attend, and students could arrive somewhat later to get the same quality of seating. If average quality increased, and the number of seats remained the same, then the student section would fill up somewhat earlier. Some form of reserved seating might be better.

5.11 Since he could have bought bundle (8, 2) when both prices were $1, but choose instead to buy bundle (4, 8), we infer that Buford prefers (4, 8) to (8, 2).

5.12 In case (1), Howard is better off in period 0, and in case (2), he is better off in period 1. In case (3), we can't be sure in which period he was better off. In the diagram for case (1), the consumption bundle chosen in period 1 must lie below the period 0 budget line, and the consumption bundle chosen in period 0 must lie above the period 1 budget line. In the diagram for case (3), the consumption bundle chosen in period 1 must lie above the period 0 budget line, and the consumption bundle chosen in period 0 must lie above the period 1 budget line.

5.13 The crucial thing to notice is that Norm's utility maximizing bundles, B^0 and B^1, always lie on the line $x_1 = x_2$ when his preferences are described by this utility function. Hence, the statements "B^0 is below the period 1 budget line" and "B^1 is above the period 0 budget line" are equivalent in the sense that either one implies the other. But, the first of these means that $P > 1$, and the second that $L > 1$. Hence $P > 1$ and $L > 1$ are equivalent statements: either one implies the other. The other results can be derived in the same fashion.

5.14 In four years time, the original $50000 would be worth $(1.1)^4 50000 = \$73205$, and the present value of the $72000 is $72000/(1.1)^4 = \$49177$. Howard should take the $50000.

5.15 a) She should ask

$$\$25000[1/(1 + i) + 1/(1 + i)^2 + 1/(1 + i)^3 + 1/(1 + i)^4]$$

or approximately $62171 if the interest rate is 10% and $52662 in it is 20%.

b) The opportunity cost of money to a farmer who must borrow it is the rate of interest at which the farmer can borrow money, and the opportunity cost of money to a farmer with lots of money in his savings account is the rate of interest earned on savings.

5.16 a) Figure 5.16 tells the story. Given the excise taxes, she buys bundle (x'_1, x'_2). The lump-sum tax is equal to $t_1 x'_1$ plus $t_2 x'_2$, which is the amount she pays in excise taxes. Hence, given the lump-sum tax, she can still buy bundle (x'_1, x'_2), and therefore can be no worse off with the lump-sum tax.

b) She will be better off with the lump sum tax if the slopes of the two budget lines are different, or if p_1/p_2 is not equal to $(p_1 + t_1)/(p_2 + t_2)$. This case is illustrated in Figure 5.16. She will be indifferent if the slopes are identical.

c) If Laura's indifference curves were kinked, and if her preferred consumption bundle was at a kink, then she might be indifferent between the taxes even when the slopes of the budget lines were not identical.

d) If good 1 one were inessential and if Laura chose to buy none of good 1 under either tax regime, then she would be indifferent between them.

FIGURE 5.16

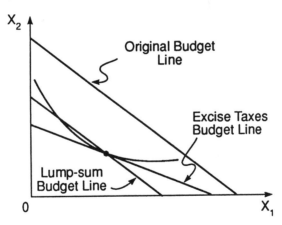

5.17 By buying 20 gallons at a time, I minimize the time cost of buying gasoline and hence maximize the income available for other goods. If I but gas 20 gallons at a time, in Becker's framework the full price per gallon is $p + w/2$ where p is the money price and w is the value of a minute to me; if I buy it 10 gallons at a time, full price is $p + w$; if I buy it 1 gallon at a time, full price is $p + 10w$.

5.18 The crucial factor (in this model) determining the choice between rail and air travel is the value of the individual's time, w per hour. For simplicity, suppose that airplanes travel at 500 mph and that trains travel at 100 mph. The full prices of a 500 mile journey by air and by rail are then $p_a + w$, and $p_r + 5w$. Air travel is cheaper if $p_a - p_r < 4w$. So people who place a high value on their time will choose to travel by air.

5.19 The lower speed limit tends to reduce miles driven because it increases the full price, which includes the time price, of driving a mile. After all, the time price in hours of driving a mile is just 1/s, where s is speed in miles per hour. The lower is s, the higher is the time price. A more sensible approach would seem to be to allow the price of gas to increase until the required reduction in consumption of gas is achieved. If all consumers were identical, this scheme would definitely be superior. But they are not identical. People who place a low value on their time will tend to prefer the first scheme, and people who place a high value on their time will tend to prefer the second scheme.

CHAPTER 6

6.1 a) Guy is indifferent between $12 and a gamble that pays $20 with probability .7 and $0 with probability .3

b) U(20) = 1, U(12) = .7, U(0) = 0

c) Guy is indifferent between the riskless prospect that pays $12 with probability 1, and the risky prospect that pays $20 with probability .7 and $0 with probability .3. The expected money value of the riskless prospect is $12, which is less than the $14 expected money value of the risky prospect. Hence, Guy is risk averse.

d) .6, .54, .7, .58, .64

e) C, E, A, D, B

6.2 The following is a utility function for Julie: U(100) = 1, U(50) = 1/2, U(10) = 0. Calculating expected utilities reveals that Julie is indifferent between the two prospects in (a), prefers the first prospect in part (b), and the second in part (c).

6.3 a) $U(5) = 4/9$

b) "C preferred to A" requires that $U(5) > 4/5$, and "A preferred to B" requires that $U(5) > 1/2$. Hence, for any person with $U(5) > 4/5$, C is preferred to A which is preferred to B. Such a person is risk averse since $4/5$ exceeds $4/9$.

c) "B preferred to A" requires that $U(5) < 1/2$, and "A preferred to C" requires that $U(5) < 4/5$. Hence, for any person with $U(5) < 1/2$, B is preferred to A which is preferred to C. Such a person could be risk averse (if $4/9 < U(5) < 1/2$), risk neutral (if $U(5) = 4/9$), or risk inclined (if $U(5) < 4/9$).

d) "B preferred to A" requires that $U(5) < 1/2$, and "C preferred to B" requires that $U(5) > 2/3$. Hence, this preference ordering is inconsistent with expected utility theory.

6.4 The expected monetary value of this game is $1 + 1 + 1 + 1 + 1 + \ldots$, the sum of an infinite string of 1s, or infinity, yet most people are unwilling to pay even $10 for the right to play this game.

6.5 When the probability of rain is $1/2$, Jane's expected profit is $12.50 if she fertilizes, and it's $12.50 if she doesn't. Hence she will be indifferent if she is risk neutral (if $U(w) = w$), will fertilize is she is risk inclined (if $U(w) = w^2$), and will not fertilize if she is risk averse (if $U(w) = w^{1/2}$).

6.6 a) 40, **b)** no, maybe, yes, **c)** $900, **d)** $800

6.7 a) $475

b) Let x denote the portion of individuals like Mike and $1 - x$ the portion of individuals like Kevin. If all individuals bought insurance, the expected payout on any policy would be $x800 + (1 - x)400$, which of course would be the competitive equilibrium price. Kevin would buy the policy only if its price was less than or equal to 475. Hence, all individuals will buy insurance at price $x800 + (1 - x)400$ if $x800 + (1 - x)400 \leq 475$, or if $x \leq 3/16$. If $x > 3/16$, only the high risk individuals like Mike will insure and they will pay $800 for the insurance. This is a case of market failure.

6.8 Yes, if some are/sex groups have significantly worse accident probabilities than others. The story is very much like the one in the previous problem where the existence of too many high risk people like Mike meant that low risk people like Kevin were driven out of the insurance market.

6.9 The three expected utilities are 5, 4, and 0.

6.10 Mr. Q would prefer the single lineup regardless of his attitude toward risk since it assures that he will get the next available teller. In addition, the single lineup system reduces the variance of time spent in the queue and hence is attractive to risk averse customers.

6.11 Ms. Q will buy the business if

$(1/2)\ln(500) + (1/2)\ln(3000) > \ln(1000)$.

But this inequality can be reduced to

$(500)^{1/2}(3000)^{1/2} > 1000$,

which reduces to

$1,500,000 > 1,000,000$.

Hence, she will buy the business.

6.12 a) He is risk averse for $w < 1$, and risk inclined for $w > 1$.

b) If he buys neither, expected utility is .9854. If he buys insurance only, expected utility is .9874. If he buys only the lottery ticket, expected utility is .9878. Finally, if he buys both, expected utility is .9898. In the last two cases, where he buys the lottery ticket, you must consider four possible outcomes: incur loss and win lottery; incur no loss and win lottery; incur loss and lose lottery; incur no loss and lose lottery.

c) He insures because he is risk averse with respect to losses and he gambles because he is risk inclined with respect to gains.

6.13 We want to show that

$pU(0) + (1 - p)U(W) < p^2 U(0) + 2p(1 - p)U(W/2) + (1 - p)^2 U(W)$

which can be reduced to

$$(1/2)U(0) + (1/2)U(W) < U(W/2)$$

This last inequality is clearly satisfied if Lucky Pierre is risk averse.

6.14 Clearly, the no-switching strategy produces the good prize with probability 1/3. Now consider the switching strategy. With probability 1/3 the good prize was behind the original curtain chosen by the contestant, and the switching strategy produces the booby prize. But, with probability 2/3, a booby prize was behind the original curtain chosen by the contestant, and in this case the switching strategy produces the good prize with certainty since the host opens the curtain concealing the other booby prize before asking the contestant if he or she wants to switch. Hence, the switching strategy produces the good prize with probability 2/3.

6.15 a) The question can be rephrased as follows: when is there a value of p such that both Arlene and Bob prefer the gamble to just eating their respective apples? For Arlene, p must be such that p > A, since p is her expected utility from entering the gamble and A is her expected utility from just eating her apple. For Bob, p must be such that 1 - p > B, or p < 1 - B. To satisfy both of these inequalities we need

$$A < p < 1 - B$$

So, if A is less than 1 - B, there is always a gamble that makes both of them better off than they are when they just eat their apples.

b) Arlene (Bob) is risk inclined if A < 1/2 (B < 1/2), and risk averse if A > 1/2 (B > 1/2). If both are risk inclined, then A is always less than 1 - B, and they will gamble, so the first statement is true. Suppose now that A = .6, so that Arlene is risk averse, and B = .3, so that Bob is risk inclined. They will gamble since .6 < 1 - .3, so the second statement is false.

6.16 See Figure 6.16. Distance AG exceeds distance AH which exceeds distance AI.

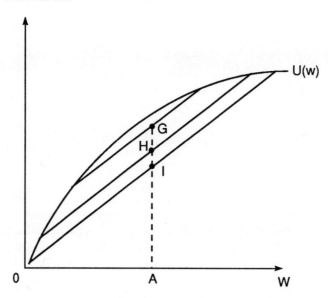

FIGURE 6.16

CHAPTER 7

7.1 See Figure 7.1.

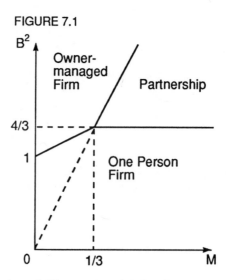

FIGURE 7.1

7.2 Race the horses with Bart riding Brett's horse and Brett riding Bart's horse.

7.3 What are the club's incentives? Suppose a tradesperson does an unsatisfactory job. It's reasonable to assume that the homeowner will leave the club, and the club's future revenue will decline by $50. Hence, in the future the club would refuse to refer club members to this particular tradesperson. But anticipating this result, the tradesperson has a clear incentive to do satisfactory work in the first place. Hence, the club solves the asymmetric information problem.

7.4 "Why does the parent company choose to sell franchises instead of hamburgers?" Imagine the organizational difficulties the firm would encounter if it attempted to manage literally thousands of restaurants. By selling franchises, the firm puts these managerial problems in the hands of thousands of independent business persons. "Why does the parent firm insist on exclusive ownership?" Apparently to avoid the sort of problem we encountered in our model of partnerships. "Why does the parent company inspect the operations of its franchisees?" The company is selling, and franchisees are buying, an image--uniform quality products in clean and healthy surroundings. The only way to produce such an image is to ensure that franchisees do produce a uniform quality product in clean and healthy surroundings. The assurance that all restaurants will be inspected and that licenses will be revoked if the restaurant is not up to snuff is the primary assurance that franchisees have that the McDonald's image will be worth something. "Why does one franchisee care about how others run their restaurants?" Because the McDonalds's image is produced collectively by all the restaurants in the chain. "Why does the parent firm agree to the restriction that it cannot sell other franchises in a specified radius?" In the absence of such a restriction the value of a franchise would be small, perhaps zero.

7.5 Designers are paid a salary because it's relatively easy to monitor them. All the publisher needs to do is to look carefully at the books under a particular designers control. Authors are not paid by salary because it's very difficult to monitor their work--to discover if a particular text is properly done would require significant effort from a number of other experts--and because it is ordinarily the author and not the publisher who knows what sort of book the market demands. Commissions are common in sales work because monitoring the effort of salespersons is often very costly. By tying the salesperson's compensation to sales made, the firm avoids the need to monitor extensively the salesperson's effort.

7.6 The key here is that the specialized equipment produced by firm O is a specific input, while the chip, produced by many firms, is a generic input. Hence, one would expect firm O to buy the generic input, assemble and sell oranges. Any other arrangement involves the tricky contractual problems raised by specific inputs.

7.7 By insisting on multiple sources for specific inputs, firms reduce the holdup problems that specific inputs create. In effect, IBM improves its bargaining position with respect to its suppliers of specific inputs by insisting on multiple sources. Security of supply is, of course, another advantage of multiple sourcing.

7.8 The compensation arrangements outlined in this problem are examples of deferred-compensation schemes. They are designed to reduce turnover by employees with firm-specific human capital. Such schemes allow a firm to economize on its investment in firm-specific human capital by reducing the number of employees it must train.

7.9 By choosing $w_1 < w'$ and $w_2 > w'$, the firm can be certain that a trained employee would never quit to take another job in period 2, and it can be sure that college bound employees will not accept jobs in period 1 only to quit and go to college in period 2. Hence this is the preferred wage profile.

CHAPTER 8

8.1 a) True b) Uncertain c) True d) True e) Uncertain f) True g) True h) True i) True

8.2 a) True b) True c) False d) False e) True f) Uncertain g) True

8.3 a) True b) Uncertain c) True d) True e) True f) Uncertain g) True

8.4 Let w denote the equivalent annual rental price, i the interest rate, and S the scrap value. The three variables are related in the following way:

$10,000 - S/(1 + i)^4 =$

$\quad w[1 + 1/(1 + i) + 1/(1 + i)^2 + 1/(1 + i)^3 + 1/(1 +)^4]$

a) $2000 b) $2398.16 c) $1000 d) $1852.47

8.5 a) A temperature differential of magnitude D

b) $800 to maintain the 20 degree temperature differential,

and $1800 to maintain the 30 degree differential

c) $400 to maintain the 20 degree temperature differential, and $900 to maintain the 30 degree differential

8.6
$TP(z_1) = z_1$ if $z_1 \leq 100$, and $TP(z_1) = 100$ if $z_1 > 100$

$MP(z_1) = 1$ if $z_1 \leq 100$, and $MP(z_1) = 0$ if $z_1 > 100$

$AP(z_1) = 1$ if $z_1 \leq 100$, and $AP(z_1) = 100/z_1$ if $z_1 > 100$

$VC(y) = y$ if $y \leq 100$

$SMC(y) = 1$ if $y \leq 100$

$STC(y) = 100 + y$ if $y \leq 100$

$SAC(y) = 1 + 100/y$ if $y \leq 100$

$AVC(y) = 1$ if $y \leq 100$

$AFC(y) = 100/y$ if $y \leq 100$

$FC = 100$

Since it is impossible to produce more than 100 units when $z_2 = 100$, these cost functions are not defined for $y > 100$.

8.7
a) $TP(z_1) = z_1^{1/3}$ $VC(z_1) = 2y^3$ $AVC(z_1) = 2y^2$ $STC(z_1) = 2y^3 + 3$

b) $TP(z_1) = 4z_1^{1/3}$ $VC(z_1) = y^3/32$ $AVC(z_1) = y^2/32$ $STC(z_1) = y^3/32 + 3$

8.8 a) Produce 5 units in the first plant and 10 in the second.

b) Produce $y/3$ in the first plant and $2y/3$ in the second.

8.9 We know that the firm minimizes cost by allocating output so that SMC is identical in the two plants. But SMC is just the price of the variable input divided by MP of the variable input. Hence, equality of SMC for the two plants implies equality of MP for the two plants.

8.10
a) $VC(y) = y$ for $y \leq 80$

$$\begin{aligned}
&= 80 + 2y && \text{for } 80 < y \le 160 \\
&= 240 + 3y && \text{for } 160 < y \le 240 \\
SMC(y) &= 1 && \text{for } y \le 80 \\
&= 2 && \text{for } 80 < y \le 160 \\
&= 3 && \text{for } 160 < y \le 240 \\
AVC(y) &= 1 && \text{for } y \le 80 \\
&= 2 + 80/y && \text{for } 80 < y \le 160 \\
&= 3 + 240/y && \text{for } 160 < y \le 240
\end{aligned}$$

b) To maximize profit produce 160 widgets and work 16 hours per day.

8.11 a) $TP(z) = 100z$ $MP(z) = 100$ $AP(z) = 100$

b) When $z = 100$, AP on the lake is equal to average product (or marginal product) on the ocean. Each of the 150 fishers has 100 fish at the end of the day for a total harvest of 15,000 fish.

c) As currently exploited, the net value of the lake is 0 fish since the 150 fishers would also catch 100 fish each if they all fished on the ocean.

d) To maximize total harvest, allocate fishers to equate marginal products. That is, allocate 25 fishers to the lake and 125 to the ocean.

e) The total harvest of fish is then 17,500 per day, for a net gain over the allocation in b) of 2,500 fish. If exploited in this fashion, the lake is worth 2,500 fish per day.

f) If the lake was owned by a profit maximizing firm, it would have to pay a wage of 100 fish, and it would hire 25 fishers. Its profit would be 2,500 fish. Hence, private property will do the trick. Similarly, if the community imposed a tax equal to 50% of the catch on the lake, only 25 fishers would fish there, and the total harvest would be 17,500 fish per day. The tax take would be 2,500 fish per day. So a tax on landings will also do the trick.

CHAPTER 9

9.1 a) True b) Uncertain c) True d) False e) Uncertain
f) Uncertain

9.2 a) True b) Uncertain c) Uncertain d) Uncertain
e) Uncertain f) True g) True h) True i) True j) True

9.3 a) False b) Uncertain c) False d) True e) False f) True

9.4 a) Certainly false b) Possibly true c) Possibly true

9.5 Her time cost is $w_3/3$ per pizza. The cost of a pizza is w_1 if she buys it from Sorento's and it is $w_2/2$ if she buys it from Pizza 222. Hence, the minimum cost of a pizza is $\min(w_1, w_2/2)$. Her cost function is then $y[w_3/3 + \min(w_1, w_2/2)]$, where y is the number of pizzas she buys and delivers.

9.6 a) $13, $13, $10

b) See Figure 9.6.

c) When $w_1 < w_2$, the cost-minimizing bundle is $(.7y, .3y)$, and when $w_1 > w_2$, it is $(.3y, .7y)$.

d) $C(w_1, w_2, y) = y[.7\min(w_1, w_2) + .3\max(w_1, w_2)]$

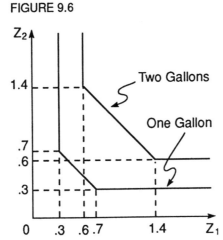

FIGURE 9.6

9.7 a) Letting z_1, z_2, z_3, and z_4 denote hours of Liz's time, gallons of gas, hours of the smaller mower, and hours of the larger mower, the production functions are $\min(z_1, 3z_2, z_3)$ and $\min(3z_1, 3z_2, 3z_4)$.

b) If Liz uses the smaller mower, the conditional input demand functions are $z_1^*=y$, $z_2^*=y/3$, and $z_3^*=y$. If she uses the larger mower, they are $z_1^*=y/3$, $z_2^*=y/3$, and $z_3^*=y/3$. The cost functions are $y[w_1+w_2/3+w_3]$ and $y[w_1/3+w_2/3+w_4/3]$.

c) The smaller mower entails lower costs if $w_1+w_2/3+w_3$ is less than $w_1/3+w_2/3+w_4/3$, or if $2w_1 < w_4-3w_3$. The price of gas is irrelevant because the gas costs per unit of lawn mowed are the same for the two mowers.

d) If the smaller mower is the cheapest way to cut grass, the price she gets for cutting a unit of lawn must exceed $w_1+w_2/3+w_3$. If the larger mower is the cheapest way to cut grass, the price she gets for cutting a unit of lawn must exceed $w_1/3+w_2/3+w_3/3$.

9.8 a) $y=(z_1^*)^a(z_2^*)^b$ and $az_2^*/bz_1^* = w_1/w_2$

b) $z_1^*=y(w_2/2w_1)^{2/3}$, $z_2^*=y(2w_1/w_2)^{1/3}$,

c) $z_1^*=y^{2/3}(w_2/w_1)^{1/2}$, $z_2^*=y^{2/3}(w_1/w_2)^{1/2}$

9.9 Consider some input bundle A, draw the associated isocost line, and an isoquant through bundle A that is locally concave. Then, if the isocost line is steeper than the isoquant at point A, bundles on the isoquant immediately to the left of A are cheaper than bundle A. If the budget line is flatter than the indifference curve at point A, bundles on the isoquant immediately to the right of A are cheaper than to bundle A. Finally, if the isocost line is tangent to the isoquant, then bundles on the isoquant immediately to the right and left of A are cheaper than A.

9.10 Figure 9.10 is relevant here. For w_1 not equal to w_2, we have the following results for both production functions:

$z_1^* = y$ and $z_2^* = 0$ if $w_1 < w_2$

$z_1^* = 0$ and $z_2^* = y$ if $w_1 > w_2$

For all input prices, we have the following cost function:

$C(w_1, w_2, y) = y\min(w_1, w_2)$

The only differences arise when $w_1 = w_2$. In this case, either of the input bundles identified above is cost minimizing for both production functions, and for the second production function, any other input bundle on the appropriate isoquant is cost minimizing.

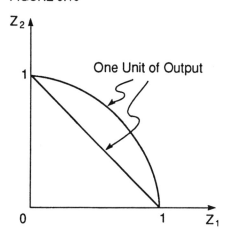

FIGURE 9.10

CHAPTER 10

10.1 a) True b) False c) True d) False, e) True f) Uncertain g) True h) True i) False j) Uncertain k) True l) Uncertain

10.2 a) Equilibrium price and quantity are $2 and 10,000. There are 200 firms in equilibrium, each producing 50 units, and earning 0 profit.

b) Equilibrium price and quantity are $2 and 14,000. There are 280 firms in equilibrium, each producing 50 units, and earning 0 profit.

c) Long-run equilibrium price and quantity will be $3 and 13,000. Short-run equilibrium price will exceed $3, and quantity will be less than 13,000.

d) Long-run equilibrium price would exceed $2, and equilibrium quantity would be less than 14,000.

10.3 Equilibrium price will fall and quantity will increase. The quantity produced by each firm will decrease and the number of firms will increase. Each firm will produce where $[LAC(y) - 100,000/y]$ is a minimum, and equilibrium price will be the value of $[LAC(y) - 100,000/y]$ at this minimum point.

10.4 a) Consumer's will prefer the lump-sum tax since it will cause price to rise by a smaller amount.

b) The excise tax will have no effect on output per firm while the lump-sum tax will result in an increase in output per firm.

10.5 $LAC(y) = 100/y + y$. The efficient scale of production is 10 crates of berries per day. Minimum average cost is 20, which is the long-run equilibrium price.

10.6 Notice that $LAC(y)$ is independent of y: average cost is identical for all levels f output. Hence there is no unique efficient scale of production. Long-run equilibrium price is equal to $(w_1 w_2/300)^{1/2}$, and equilibrium quantity is just the quantity demanded at this price. Since there is no unique efficient scale, the sizes and number of firms in equilibrium are indeterminate.

10.7 a) The firm will produce 10 units and its profit will be -$300. It is possible, though clearly not necessary, that this price is a long-run equilibrium price and that this firm has the wrong scale of production.

b) $y^* = (p - 30)/2$

c) The firm makes zero profit when price is $70. This price may or may not be a long-run equilibrium price.

10.8 a) $y = 1000 - 5p$

b) $y^* = (p - 10)/2$

c) $y = 5p - 50$

d) Equilibrium price and quantity are 105 and 475.

e) Equilibrium price and quantity are 110 and 450.

10.9 a) Equilibrium price in both the short and long run will rise to the level at which 4/5 of the pre-quota equilibrium quantity will be demanded.

b) In the short run, quantity produced by a typical producer will fall to 4000 eggs per day. In the long run some farmers will go out of business and others will buy their quota. In the new long run equilibrium, each farm will again produce 5000 eggs per day.

c) The number of firms will fall to 4/5 the original number.

d) Let D denote the increase in the price of an egg caused by the quota. Then, assuming that everyone expects the future to be identical to the present, the price of the right to produce one egg a day will be the present value of D over an infinite horizon.

e) The original egg farmers who are simply given valuable quota are clearly better off. Future farmers will be no better off since they will have to buy quota. Given the price they pay, they will be earning a zero profit.

f) There is a clear incentive for "bootlegging" eggs and for a black market in eggs.

g) The more inelastic is the demand for eggs the more attractive is any given quota system to incumbent egg producers.

CHAPTER 11

11.1 a) The profit maximizing price is $70 per book, 6000 books will be sold, profit will be $180,000, and the author's royalty will be $120,000.

b) The profit maximizing price is $60 per book, 8000 books will be sold, profit will be $320,000, the author's share of the profit will be $128,000, and the publisher's share will be $192,000. Notice that the author, the publisher, and the student are all better off than in part a.

c) The problem with the original agreement is that the $20 royalty fee per book is not really a cost of production. It is just a way to compensate the author. As we have seen, profit sharing is a better way to compensate the author.

11.2 Adults will pay the highest price and children the lowest. If children pay $2, then students pay $20/9, adults pay $10/3, and marginal cost is $5/3.

11.3 a) Marginal cost is $10, the profit maximizing output is 50 units, the profit maximizing price is $60, and profit is $2500 - F$.

b) Price is driven down to $60 when the monopolist produces 50 units, and price drops by $1 for every unit the entrant produces.

c) The entrant would produce 25 units, price would be $35, and the entrant's profit would be $625 - F.

d) The market is a natural monopoly for any value of F greater than or equal to than $625.

11.4 There is a clear economic case for offering patent protection before new products are invented since patent protection acts as an incentive to create new, socially valuable products. But there is no obvious economic case for extending patents on products that have already been created. The primary implications of such an extension would appear to be a continued high price for the product and continued monopoly inefficiency.

11.5 a) In effect the tax raises the monopolist's marginal cost by the amount of the tax, t.

b) The following table gives the relevant information for various values of t:

t	output	price	profit
0	19	105	1805
10	18	110	1670
20	17	115	1445
30	16	120	1280

11.6 Consider the Expo strategy. The $100 ticket enables the holder to avoid time spent in queues, while the $20 ticket entails a time price--time spent in queues times the value the individual places on his or her time. People who place a high value on their time will buy the $100 ticket and those who place a low value on their time will buy the $20 ticket. For this to be a profitable strategy, it is necessary but not sufficient that the demand for tickets of the former group be less price elastic than demand of the latter group.

11.7 Suppose there are two types of readers (or film buffs). One type is impatient and wants to read the very latest books while the other patient and content to wait a few months before reading a newly released book. If demand for the impatient group is more price inelastic than demand for the patient group, then this may be a profitable way to price discriminate. Market segmentation is achieved by self-selection.

11.8 a) The profit maximizing quantity and price are 30 and $140.

c) With a $100 price ceiling, the profit maximizing price and quantity are $100 and 50. With a $160 price ceiling the profit maximizing quantity and price are 30 and $140.

d) The efficient solution is price equal to $80 and quantity equal to 60 units. A price ceiling equal to $80.01 will get the monopolist to produce nearly 60 units at the price ceiling. If the price ceiling is exactly $80, however, the monopolist is content with any positive output, or no output at all.

11.9 a) The profit maximizing prices are $45 and $60, and maximized profit is $382.50.

b) There are many such schemes, so the following is just one of many correct answers. The two prices are $45 and $30, and the higher price applies to the first 4.5 units. Relative to a), the increase in profit is 4.5 times $15.

c) $\quad p = 90 - 10y$ and $MR = 90 - 20y \quad$ if $y \leq 3$

$\quad\quad p = 70 - 10y/3$ and $MR = 70 - 20y/3 \quad$ if $y > 3$

$\quad\quad p^* = \$35$ and maximized profit $= \$367.50$

11.10 If $y \leq 10$, the possibility of import competition means that the Nickel Company can't charge a price higher than $90; hence its marginal revenue function is $90 for $y \leq 10$. When $y = 20$, marginal revenue in the Canadian market is $60, the competitive price in the world market. For $y > 20$, the Nickel Company sells 20 units in the Canadian market at a price of $80, and $y - 20$ in the world market at a price of $60. Its marginal revenue function is $60 for $y > 20$. If $10 < y \leq 20$, then the Nickel Company sells only in the Canadian market at a price equal to $100 - y$, and its marginal revenue function is $100 - 2y$.

a) If $a = 2$, marginal revenue equals marginal cost when $y = 30$, and the Company sells 20 units in Canada at price $80, and 10 units in the international market at price $60. Its revenue is $2200 and its costs (equal to the area under the marginal cost function and above the horizontal axis from 0 to 30 units) are $900. Its profit is then $1300.

b) If a = 14/3, it sells 15 units in the Canadian market at price $85 and none in the international market. Its revenue is $1275 and its cost is $525, for a profit of $750.

c) If a = 30, it sells 3 units in the Canadian market at price $90, and its revenue is $270. Its costs are $135 and its profit is $135.

11.11 Total revenue is $160y - y^2/2$, average revenue is $160 - y/2$, and marginal revenue is $160 - y$.

CHAPTER 12

12.1 a) Output, price, and profit are 360 units, $460, and $64,800.

b) Given n firms, output of a representative firm, equilibrium price, and profit of a representative firm are $720[n/(n+1)]$, $\$(460+100n)/(n+1)$, $\$259200/(n+1)^2$.

c) In the symmetric collusive equilibrium each firm produces 180 units and earns $32,400 in profit. The violator should produce 270 units, and the inducement to violate the agreement is then $4,050.

d) The limit output is 560 units, the limit price is $180, and the monopolist's profit is $44,800 - $3200.

e) Just 2 firms will enter since the profit of a third would be $16,200 - $20,000 which is negative. Each firm will earn profit equal to $28,800 - $20,000 = $8800.

f) Three firms will enter, and each will earn a profit equal to $21,600 - $20,000 = $1600.

g) Just one firm will enter and its profit will be $44,800.

12.2 Under the common property institution we have the following payoff matrix:

	R	E
R	(150, 150)	(75, 165)
E	(165, 75)	(90, 90)

And under the private property institution we have the

following payoff matrix:

```
         R            E
R    (150, 150)   (150, 90)

E    (90, 150)    (90, 90)
```

In the first game the dominant strategy is E and in the second it is R.

12.3 The profit maximizing price and quantity are $1000 and 1000, a combination that generates revenue of $1,000,000. When K is 600,000, there will be 1 firm operating at capacity; when K is 300,000, there will be 3 firms operating at 1/3 capacity; when K is 150,000, there will be 6 firms operating at 1/6 capacity.

12.4 a) The best response functions are $y_1 = (100 - y_2)/3$, and $y_2 = (100 - y_1)/3$.

b) Each firm will produce 25 units in equilibrium, price will be $50, and each firm's profit will be $937.50.

12.5 Let A be the amount spent by the incumbent firm on advertising prior to entry. If quantity demanded from an entrant, given its price and the incumbent's price, is negatively related to A, then advertising is a barrier to entry.

12.6 An infinite inventory would mean a zero marginal cost of production, and a finite inventory would mean a zero marginal cost for the amount held in inventory. If, in the post entry equilibrium, the entrant's profit is negatively related to the incumbent's marginal cost, then inventories are a barrier to entry.

12.7 a) The best response functions are $y_1 = (105 - y_2)/2$, and $y_2 = (90 - y_1)/2$. Equilibrium quantities are $x_1 = 40$, and $x_2 = 25$. Equilibrium price is $55.

b) The equilibrium prices are $p_1 = \$29.99$ and $p_2 = \$30.00$. Firm 1 makes all the sales, its profit per unit sold is $14.99, and it sells 90.01 units.

12.8 First of all, learning by doing can constitute a barrier to entry for the reason outlined in question 6: the lower is an incumbent firm's marginal cost, the more aggressive it may be toward new entrants. Second, firms may have an incentive to produce abnormally large quantities early on in order to get down the learning curve, thereby realizing lower marginal costs and hence making it more difficult for other firms to enter.

CHAPTER 13

13.1 a) Notice first that transport costs are effectively $.20 per mile. At identical prices, each sells 500 cones. When Jones' price is $1 and Smith's is $1.40, Jones sells 600 cones and Smith sells 400.

b) Use the demand functions in part c).

c) The demand functions are

$$y_1 = 500 + 250(p_2 - p_1)$$
$$y_2 = 500 + 250(p_1 - p_2)$$

We assume that the difference in the two prices does not exceed $2.

d) $p_1 = 2 + p_2 - y_1/250$ and $MR_1 = 2 + p_2 - y_1/125$

e) Equilibrium prices are each $3 and quantities are each 500. Profit per firm is $1000 - $800 = $200 per day.

f) Given that Smith and Jones charge $3 per cone, the profit maximizing price for Llewelyn is $2.50, and Llewelyn's profit would be $1125 - $800 = $325.

g) It's difficult to tell exactly what will happen. We can be sure of one thing, however--Smith and Jones will not continue to charge $3 per cone. Thus the profit calculation in part f) should not lead Llewelyn to anticipate a profit of $325 per day.

CHAPTER 14

14.1 Efficiency in the allocation of any input requires that marginal factor cost be equal to value of the marginal product in all of the firms using the input. This condition is satisfied if all markets, input and output, are competitive. As Figure 14.16 reveals, the condition is not satisfied if any market is imperfectly competitive.

14.2 a) His marginal revenue function is $1.60 - .02y$, 60 cans is the profit maximizing output, the price is $1 per can, and his profit is $36 per ballgame.

b) His one costly input is the Coke he buys. Letting z denote quantity of Coke, $MRP(z) = 1.60 - .02z$ since the marginal product of this input is 1. This is, of course, Walley's input demand function and he maximizes profit by choosing z so that $MRP(z)$ is equal to the input price. If the input price is $.40 per can, he buys 60 cans, and if it is $.60 per can he buys 50 cans.

14.3 a) $MRP(z) = 1000 - 20z$ and $ARP(z) = 1000 - 10z$. $MRP(z)$ is the firm's demand function. The firm will use 48 units when the input price is $40 and 47 units when it is $60. The profit maximizing rule for this input market is to choose z so that w is equal MRP:

$$w = p(100 - 2z)$$

where p is price of the firm's output.

b) Marginal cost is just input price divided by marginal product. Hence, setting marginal cost equal to price we get

$$w/(100 - 2z) = p$$

as the profit maximizing rule, which is equivalent to the profit maximizing rule in the input market.

c) The input demand function is $p(100 - 2z)$. The firm will choose z so that $w = p(100 - 2z)$.

14.4 Let w_1 and w_2 be the discriminatory wages, with $w_1 > w_2$. In the model of monopsony discrimination, effective equal pay for equal work legislation will eliminate the employer's ability to discriminate. Hence all wages will be equal in the monopsony equilibrium. The equilibrium wage will be larger than w_2 and smaller than w_1, employment of group 2 will increase, and employment of group 1 will decrease. The real difficulty is making the legislation effective since the employer has a profit incentive to disguise discrimination by, for example, labeling the same job done by men and women in different ways. The primary difficulty with equal pay for work of equal value is the problem that an external enforcer would have in observing "value." The appropriate concept of value would seem to be marginal revenue product. How could an external enforcer accurately observe marginal revenue product? In practice, two jobs are often deemed to produce equal value if they require roughly equivalent training and education. Of course, this does not mean that the marginal revenue products of the two jobs are equal. Neither sort of legislation is necessary when all labor markets are competitive since equal pay for equal work and equal pay for work of equal value are properties of the competitive equilibrium.

14.5 a) To maximize profit $z_1 = 45$, $w_1 = 55$, $z_2 = 50$, and $w_2 = 50$. The firm's profit is $(45)^2 + (50)^2 = 4525$.

b) $w = z$ if $z \leq 10$, $w = 5 + z/2$ if $z > 10$. To maximize profit, $z = 95$, $w = 52.50$, and the firm's profit is 4512.50.

c) The firm is clearly worse off in b). Workers from subgroup 1 are worse of and workers from subgroup 2 are better off.

14.6 Consider the choice of a member of group A (or B) between one firm in which all other employees are members of group A (or B), and another in which some employees are members of group B (or A), and let w_1 and w_2 be the corresponding reservation wages. The preferences outlined in the problem imply that $w_1 < w_2$--a wage premium is required to induce the individual to work with employees who are members of the other group. Hence any firm which is integrated will have to pay more for its labor than a segregated firm. If the industry is competitive, only segregated firms will survive. There will be no wage differentials between the groups, however, if employers are not bigoted. If, for example,the wage for group A exceeded the wage for group B, employers' demand for group B would rise and their demand for group A would fall until wage equality was established.

14.7 In equilibrium, $z_1 = 60$, $z_2 = 40$, $w_1 = 80$, and $w_2 = 120$.

14.8 a) Consider any one of the suppliers: for each demander, the maximum price is $200 minus transport costs from the supplier's location to the demander's location.

b,c) Mile 487.5 is equidistant from the two suppliers. The firm located at mile 0 buys the coal from suppliers to the left of this point, and pays one cent more than the maximum price the other firm is willing to pay. Similarly, the firm located at mile 975 buys the coal from suppliers to the right of this point, and pays one cent more than the maximum price the other firm is willing to pay.

14.9 a) Firm A will offer w = $50 and firm B will supply 50 units.

b) Firm B will offer w = $120 and A will demand 40 units.

c) Firm C would produce 66 and 2/3 units.

14.10 Suppose the supply of labor to the labor broker is $a + bz$, where a and b are positive constants. The marginal factor cost to the labor broker is $a + 2bz$. Suppose that the demand for labor is $c - dz$, where c and d are positive constants and $c > a$. Then marginal revenue to the labor broker is $c - 2dz$. The broker will choose z so that marginal factor cost is equal to marginal revenue, employing $z^* = (c - a)/(2(b + d))$. Then $w_1 = a + bz^*$, and $w_2 = c - dz^*$.

CHAPTER 15

15.1 When good 1 is monopolized, efficiency in product mix is violated because the common value of MRS exceeds MRT. Hence too little of good 1 is produced. By subsidizing the production of good 1, or taxing the production of good 2, we can cause the production of good 1 to increase and the production of good 2 to decrease. Choosing the value of the tax or the subsidy appropriately, we can establish equality of MRS and MRT in general equilibrium.

15.2 Producers in the region where input 1 is taxed will use an input bundle where MRTS = $(w_1 + t)/w_2$; producers in the other region will use a bundle where MRTS = w_1/w_2. Hence the condition for efficiency in production is not satisfied. Notice that the economy is inside its production possibilities frontier in this case.

15.3 Unless the degree of monopsony power is identical for all firms, MRTS will not be identical for all firms. Hence, the economy will not be efficient in production: it will be inside its production possibilities frontier.

CHAPTER 16

16.1 (a) Rawl's difference principle implies that A is the preferred institution.

(b) Institution B maximizes expected utility.

(c) Individuals 1 and 2 both prefer institution C to either B or A. Hence, with majority rule and self-interested voters, institution C will be chosen.

16.2 (a) She will hire 60 workers at wage rate $40.

(b) Given Hilary's demand for labor, if the wage rate is less than $50, an increase in the wage rate will cause Hilary to hire more workers.

(c) The highest wage consistent with not reducing employment is $70.

16.3 (a) The equilibrium wage rate is 74.50, 149 workers are allocated to sector 1, and 51 are allocated to sector 2.

(b) The wage in sector 2 will be 49 and 102 workers will be in this sector.

(c) There will be 140 workers chasing 98 jobs in sector 1, so in any one period there will be 42 unemployed workers, or a 21% unemployment rate. Expected earnings wage in any period will be 70 in sector 1, equal to the certain wage in sector 2.

16.4 (1) Lump sum transfers are consistent with Pareto-optimality because they do not distort market prices.

(2) They are impractical as a means of redistributing income or wealth because, for any practical set of guidelines determining who is to receive a transfer, there are actions which some people can take that would qualify them for the transfer. This, of course, means that, for these individuals, the transfers are conditional; that is, they are not lumpsum transfers.

(3) The difficulty with conditional transfers or taxes is that they result in an inefficient product mix in general equilibrium. In the presence of a conditional transfer, the price of leisure to individuals is not equal to the price of

labor to firms, which results in an inefficient product mix. Unconditional transfers and taxes do not produce this sort of distortion.

16.5 If the demand for services is price inelastic, then an increase in the price of professional services increases the total income that members of the profession can earn and decreases the quantity of services demanded. Thus, immediately after the price increase, existing professionals will earn more and work less. But this makes the profession more attractive, and more people will enter it, reducing average income and average hours worked by each professional. If existing professionals and new professionals have identical preferences, the entry of new professionals will cease only when the profession is as attractive as it was before the price increase. In this case in the long run professionals are not better off, but society is worse off because each professional is underemployed. Now consider entry standards. If existing professionals do not have to meet higher entry standards, then they have a clear private incentive to increase entry standards. The increase in standards will make the profession less attractive to new entrants, and the supply of professional services will shift leftward, increasing the price of professional services.

CHAPTER 17

17.1 These interpretations are straightforward.

17.2 a) Type 1 firms emit 100 units of gunk and type 2 firms emit 150 units. In total the 20 firms emit 2500 units of gunk.

b) A tax equal to $75 per unit of gunk will do the job. Assuming that all firms are perfect competitors in their output markets, the 1000 units of gunk are efficiently allocated since the value of the marginal product of gunk is identical in all firms.

c) The aggregate supply is 1000 units and aggregate demand is $2500 - 20w$, where w is the price the right to emit 1 unit of gunk. Equilibrium price is $75, and the allocation of the 1000 units to the 20 firms is identical to the allocation in part b).

d) In this case the gunk emission rights are inefficiently allocated, since the emission rights are not allocated to their most productive uses.

17.3 a) 15 units.

b) Given y_1, individual 2 will choose y_2 to satisfy the following equation:

$$20 - y_1 - y_2^* = 10, \text{ or } y_2^* = 10 - y_1.$$

Similarly, individual 1 will choose

$$y_1^* = 10 - y_2.$$

Adding y_1^* and y_2^*, we get 10 units supplied. Hence, if 10 units are supplied, neither individual will want to supply more or less mosquito control and we therefore have a Nash equilibrium. Notice that the Nash equilibrium is not unique.

c) The socially optimal quantity satisfies

$$100(20 - y) = 10$$

Thus, 19.9 units of mosquito control is socially optimal. Let S denote the quantity supplied by all individuals other than i. Then individual i will supply

$$y_i^* = 10 - S$$

Hence, given quantity supplied by all other individuals, each individual will supply just enough so that aggregate supply is 10 units, Thus, any situation in which aggregate supply is 10 units is a Nash equilibrium.

d) Begin by supposing that one naive individual will supply 10 units. What will all the others do? Free ride by supplying nothing.

17.4 In the first case we need $B_A + B_B + B_C < K$, and B_A and B_B greater than $K/3$. Observe that $B_B + B_C < 2K/3$; otherwise, $B_A + B_B + B_C$ would exceed K since B_A necessarily exceeds $K/3$. We must find a bribe S such that $S > B_B - K/3$ and $S < K/3 - B_C$, which requires only that $K/3 - B_C > B_B - K/3$, or that $B_B + B_C < 2K/3$. Hence there is a bribe which C would offer to B to vote against the project and which B would accept. Now suppose that $B_A + B_B + B_C > K$, and that only A and B would vote for the project. This does not rule out the possibility that $B_B + B_C < 2K/3$; hence C might be able to bribe B to vote against the project. But A would be willing to offer an even larger bribe, T. The largest bribe that C would offer B is $K/3 - B_C$, in which case B's net benefit is $K/3 - B_C$. If A offers B a bribe T to vote for the project, then B's net benefit is $B_B - K/3 + T$. Hence, T must be larger than $2K/3 - B_B - B_C$ for B to prefer A's bribe to C's maximum bribe. The largest bribe A would be willing to offer is $T = B_A - K/3$. We must then show that $B_A - K/3$ exceeds $2K/3 - B_B - B_C$, which requires only that $B_A + B_B + B_C > K$. Such bribes ensure that the cost-benefit efficient solutions implemented.

Classroom Experiments

Many instructors like the idea of using classroom experiments in teaching microeconomics because the experiments grab students' attention and get them actively involved in particular issues in microeconomics. The problem is that devising and running these experiments means extra preparation time for the instructor--time that is sometimes simply not available. As a result, some instructors may decide not to use classroom experiments as a teaching aid--even though they like the idea.

These experiments are designed to remedy that problem. We have developed a set of ten experiments to accompany our textbook, Microeconomics, second edition. Each experiment is divided into two parts. First, a note to the instructor explains when and how to implement the experiment. Second, tear-out instruction sheets for students are provided. These may be photocopied and handed out to students. (NOTE: This material is copyrighted. We give permission for reproduction free of charge only to users of Eaton and Eaton Microeconomics.) Of course, we would be delighted to have suggestions for improvements and additions to this manual from one and all. The more feedback we get, the more usable and pertinent it will become.*

A note on presenting the experiments in class. It is important to tell students very clearly that these experiments will not be used for research purposes by anyone involved. Once they know that these experiments are strictly classroom aids, students are generally much more cooperative experimental subjects. Finally, even though we have provided seemingly self-explanatory instructions to students for every experiment, you must still take time before they begin the experiment to review the instructions and ask for any questions.

---

* We are indebted to Jack Knetsch for comments on earlier versions of these experiments.

NOTE TO THE INSTRUCTOR
Experiments 1 and 2
Chapter 1 of *Microeconomics* by Eaton and Eaton

These experiments, which capture some of the essential features of the Hotelling model of spatial competition, are designed to be used in conjunction with Chapter 1. It takes approximately 15 minutes of class time to run each experiment and perhaps 25 minutes to tabulate the results for a class of 50 students. We suggest that you conduct the experiments in the first lecture of your course and discuss the results after you have derived the minimally-differentiated equilibrium of the Hotelling model.

In each experiment Player One first chooses a 1, 2, 3, 4, or 5. Knowing Player One's choice, Player Two then chooses a 1, 2, 3, 4 or 5. The players are then asked to imagine that a host randomly selects one of these integers from a density function known to the players and then pays the player whose choice is closer to the host's selection $100. If both choices are equally close to the host's selection, then each player receives $50.

In Experiment 1 the density function is uniform and the equilibrium strategies are that Player One chooses 3 and Player Two chooses 3. In Experiment 2, the density function is nonuniform and the equilibrium strategies are that Player One chooses 2 and Player Two chooses 2.

Before you begin, carefully explain that the results of the experiments are not for any research purpose but are for classroom use only. To implement either experiment, make the required number of copies of the instructions. Then divide students into pairs, giving one student from each pair the instructions for Player One and the other student the instructions for Player Two. If you decide to perform both experiments, we suggest that you do so at the same time, using half of the students for Experiment 1 and half for Experiment 2. If you do perform them simultaneously, check to see that the two students in each pair have the instructions for the same experiment. After students have read the instructions and before they have made their choices, explain the instructions to the class as a whole and ask for questions.

In discussing the results with your class, begin by showing how the choices of numbers in the experiments correspond to the choices of locations in the Hotelling model. It is useful to focus separately on the two versions of the experiment and, within each version, to focus separately on the choices of the the players who choose (or move) first and those who choose second. For the second choices, report the numbers (and the percentages) of players who did and did not choose the strategy that maximized their expected payoffs, given the integer chosen by the first player. For the first choices, report the numbers of players who chose each of the five integers.

Copyright © 1991 W. H. Freeman and Company. All rights reserved.

Name: _____

INSTRUCTIONS FOR PLAYER ONE
Experiment 1
Chapter 1 of <u>Microeconomics</u> by Eaton and Eaton

The following game of chance involves two players and an imaginary game show host with $100 in prize money. You are Player One. You must choose one of the five integers 1, 2, 3, 4 or 5. When you have made your choice, you will record it on Player Two's instruction sheet so that he/she knows your choice before making his/her choice. After you have recorded your choice, Player Two will then choose one of the same five integers and record that choice on his/her instruction sheet. (He/she is allowed to choose the same number that you chose or a different number.)

The imaginary host has five ping-pong balls in a brown paper bag. One ball has a "1" written on it, one has a "2," one has a "3," one has a "4," and one has a "5." After you and your opponent have made your choices, imagine that the host randomly selects one of the balls from the paper bag. Imagine, too, that he will pay $100 to the player whose chosen integer is closer to the one selected from the bag and will pay nothing to the other player. If both choices are equally close to the selected integer, the host will pay each player $50. For example, if you chose 4 and your opponent chose 2, you would get $100 if the host selected a 4 or 5, $50 if the host selected a 3, and nothing if the host selected a 1 or a 2.

Think about the game for a few minutes, and then record your choice at the bottom of Player Two's instruction sheet.

Copyright © 1991 W. H. Freeman and Company. All rights reserved.

Name: _____

INSTRUCTIONS FOR PLAYER TWO
Experiment 1
Chapter 1 of <u>Microeconomics</u> by Eaton and Eaton

The following game of chance involves two players and an imaginary game show host with $100 in prize money. You are Player Two. Player One will first choose one of the five integers 1, 2, 3, 4 or 5, and then record his/her choice at the bottom of your instruction sheet. You will then choose one of the same five integers and record your choice at the bottom of this sheet. (You are allowed to choose the same number that Player One chose or a different number.)

The imaginary host has five ping-pong balls in a paper bag. One ball has a "1" written on it, one has a "2," one has a "3," one has a "4," and one has a "5." After you and your opponent have made your choices, imagine that the host randomly selects one of the balls from the paper bag. Imagine, too, that he will pay $100 to the player whose chosen integer is closer to the one selected from the bag and will pay nothing to the other player. If both choices are equally close to the selected integer, the host will pay each player $50. For example, if you chose 4 and your opponent chose 2, you would get $100 if the host selected a 4 or 5, $50 if the host selected a 3, and nothing if the host selected a 1 or a 2.

After Player One records his/her choice in the space provided below, make your choice and record it.

Player One's Choice   _____

Player Two's Choice   _____

Copyright © 1991 W. H. Freeman and Company. All rights reserved.

Name: _____

INSTRUCTIONS FOR PLAYER ONE
Experiment 2
Chapter 1 of *Microeconomics* by Eaton and Eaton

The following game of chance involves two players and an imaginary game show host with $100 in prize money. You are Player One. You must choose one of the five integers 1, 2, 3, 4 or 5. When you have made your choice, you will record it on Player Two's instruction sheet so that he/she knows your choice before making his/her choice. After you have recorded your choice, Player Two then will choose one of the same five integers and record that choice on his/her instruction sheet. (He/she is allowed to choose the same number that you chose or a different number.)

The imaginary host has seven ping-pong balls in a paper bag. Two of the balls are labeled "1" and two are labeled "2." One ball is labeled "3," one is labeled "4," and one is labeled "5." After you and your opponent have made your choices, imagine that the host randomly selects one of the balls from the paper bag. Imagine, too, that he will pay $100 to the player whose chosen integer is closer to the one selected from the bag and will pay nothing to the other player. If both choices are equally close to the selected integer, the host will pay each player $50. For example, if you chose 4 and your opponent chose 2, you would get $100 if the host selected a 4 or 5, $50 if the host selected a 3, and nothing if the host selected a 1 or a 2.

Think about the game for a few minutes, and then record your choice at the bottom of Player Two's instruction sheet.

Copyright © 1991 W. H. Freeman and Company. All rights reserved.

Name: _____

INSTRUCTIONS FOR PLAYER TWO
Experiment 2
Chapter 1 of <u>Microeconomics</u> by Eaton and Eaton

The following game of chance involves two players and an imaginary game show host with $100 in prize money. You are Player Two. Player One will first choose one of the five integers 1, 2, 3, 4 or 5, and then record his/her choice at the bottom of your instruction sheet. You will then choose one of the same five integers and record your choice at the bottom of this sheet. (You are allowed to choose the same number that Player One chose or a different number.)

The imaginary host has seven ping-pong balls in a paper bag. Two of the balls are labeled "1" and two are labeled "2." One ball is labeled "3," one is labeled "4," and one is labeled "5." After you and your opponent have made your choices, imagine that the host randomly selects one of the balls from the paper bag. Imagine, too, that he will pay $100 to the player whose chosen integer is closer to the one selected from the bag and will pay nothing to the other player. If both choices are equally close to the selected integer, the host will pay each player $50. For example, if you chose 4 and your opponent chose 2, you would get $100 if the host selected a 4 or 5, $50 if the host selected a 3, and nothing if the host selected a 1 or a 2.

After Player One records his/her choice in the space provided below, make your choice and record it.

Player One's Choice _____

Player Two's Choice _____

Copyright © 1991 W. H. Freeman and Company. All rights reserved.

NOTE TO THE INSTRUCTOR
Experiment 3
Chapters 2 or 5 of **Microeconomics** by Eaton and Eaton

This common property experiment is designed to illustrate the central role institutions play in organizing economic activity. It can be used in conjunction with either Chapter 2 or Chapter 5. It takes approximately 15 minutes of class time to perform the experiment and about 30 minutes to tabulate results for a class of 50.

There are four versions of the experiment, involving 1, 2, 3, and 5 players. (Because Game 1 involves only one player and therefore raises no common property issues, the maximizing outcome is obvious, and you may not want to conduct this experiment.) In each version a player imagines that he/she is given $90 and instructed to keep it or put it in a common pool. For every $90 that is put in the common pool, an imaginary experimenter adds another $60 and then divides the money in the common pool among all the players.

The game mimicks a two-period common-property fishery in which (1) each individual initially has 90 fish; (2) a fish returned to the common pool produces 5/3 fish tomorrow; and (3) a fish today is a perfect substitute for a fish tomorrow. As the number of players in the experiment increases, each individual's property rights in the fish that he/she returns to the common pool are progressively attenuated. In a typical experiment this attenuation of property rights is reflected by fewer and fewer players returning "fish" to the common pool. Used in conjunction with Chapter 2, the experiment illustrates the sometimes useful role of private property in directing resources to their most valuable use. Common property problems are discussed in some detail in Chapter 5. Used in conjunction with Chapter 5, the experiment illustrates the nature of such problems.

Before you begin the experiment, carefully explain that the results of the experiment are **not** for any research purpose but are for classroom use **only**. To implement the experiment, make the required number of copies of the instructions and randomly give each student instructions for one of the four experiments. To inhibit communication among students, form the groups themselves after students have expressed their choices. Indeed, if you choose to report only the aggregate results to your students, you do not need to actually form the groups. However, if you choose to report the individual payoffs to students, you will need to form the groups. After students have read the instructions and before they have made their choices, explain the instructions to the class as a whole and ask for questions.

Copyright © 1991 W. H. Freeman and Company. All rights reserved.

Name: _____

INSTRUCTIONS FOR GAME 1
Experiment 3
Chapters 2 or 5 of <u>Microeconomics</u> by Eaton and Eaton

The following imaginary game involves you and a host with lots of prize money. Imagine that the host gives you $90 and an envelope, telling you that you can keep the $90 or put all the money into the envelope. If you put the $90 in the envelope, the host will add $60 to it, and give the whole $150 back to you. If you do not put the $90 in the envelope, the host will add nothing to it, and you will get just $90. Indicate the choice you would make by a check mark.

_____ **I would keep the $90.**

_____ **I would put the $90 in the envelope.**

Copyright © 1991 W. H. Freeman and Company. All rights reserved.

The following tables facilitate the calculation of individual payoffs for Games 2, 3, and 4. The number n is the number of individuals who display cooperative behavior by putting their $150 in the common pool. The entries in rows labeled C are the payoffs to cooperative behavior and the entries in rows labeled N are the payoffs to noncooperative behavior.

Game 2

	n = 0	n = 1	n = 2
C	–	75	150
N	90	165	–

Game 3

	n = 0	n = 1	n = 2	n = 3
C	–	50	100	150
N	90	140	190	–

Game 4

	n = 0	n = 1	n = 2	n = 3	n = 4	n = 5
C	–	30	60	90	120	150
N	90	120	150	180	210	–

In reporting aggregate results it is useful to calculate the expected payoffs to cooperative and to noncooperative behavior. Let N be the <u>total</u> number of students who played a particular game and let n be the number who displayed cooperative behavior. The expected payoff to cooperative behavior is $150n/N$, and the expected payoff to noncooperative behavior is $90 + 150n/N$.

Copyright © 1991 W. H. Freeman and Company. All rights reserved.

Name: _____

INSTRUCTIONS FOR GAME 2
Experiment 3
Chapters 2 or 5 of <u>Microeconomics</u> by Eaton and Eaton

The following imaginary game involves two players and a host with lots of prize money. Imagine that the players are initially in separate rooms. The host first gives each player $90 and an envelope, telling each that he/she can either keep the $90 or put all the money into the envelope. The two players and the host then go to a common room where the host collects the envelopes and counts the money. For every $90 she finds, she adds $60 and then divides the total sum equally between the two players.

Now imagine that you are one of the two players in this game. You must choose to keep the $90 or put it all in your envelope. Indicate the choice you would make by a check mark.

_____ **I would keep the $90**

_____ **I would put the $90 in the envelope.**

Copyright © 1991 W. H. Freeman and Company. All rights reserved.

Name: _____

INSTRUCTIONS FOR GAME 3
Experiment 3
Chapters 2 or 5 of <u>Microeconomics</u> by Eaton and Eaton

The following imaginary game involves three players and a host with lots of prize money. Imagine that the players are initially in separate rooms. The host first gives each player $90 and an envelope, telling each that he/she can either keep the $90 or put all the money into the envelope. The three players and the host then go to a common room where the host collects the envelopes and counts the money. For every $90 she finds, she adds $60 and then divides the total sum equally among the three players.

Now imagine that you are one of the three players in this game. You must choose to keep the $90 or put it all in your envelope. Indicate the choice you would make by a check mark.

_____ I would keep the $90.

_____ I would put the $90 in the envelope.

Copyright © 1991 W. H. Freeman and Company. All rights reserved.

Name: _____

INSTRUCTIONS FOR GAME 4
Experiment 3
Chapters 2 or 5 of <u>Microeconomics</u> by Eaton and Eaton

The following imaginary game involves five players and a host with lots of prize money. Imagine that the players are initially in separate rooms. The host first gives each player $90 and an envelope, telling each that he/she can either keep the $90 or put all the money into the envelope. The five players and the host then go to a common room where the host collects the envelopes and counts the money. For every $90 she finds, she adds $60 and then divides the total sum equally among the five players.

Now imagine that you are one of the five players in this game. You must choose to keep the $90 or put it all in your envelope. Indicate the choice you would make by a check mark.

_____ I **would keep the $90.**

_____ I **would put the $90 in the envelope.**

Copyright © 1991 W. H. Freeman and Company. All rights reserved.

NOTE TO THE INSTRUCTOR
Experiment 4
Chapter 3 of **Microeconomics** by Eaton and Eaton

This experiment, which is designed to give students an indication of the extent to which expressed preferences are consistent with the transitivity assumption, is helpful in introducing students to the issues raised in Chapter 3. It takes approximately 10 minutes of class time to perform the experiment and about 20 minutes to tabulate results for a class of 50 students. We suggest that you use the experiment in the first lecture on the theory of self-interest and that you report the results in the second lecture.

The objective of the experiment is necessarily modest since it is very time-intensive to discover intransitivities in expressed preferences. The first, seventh, and twelfth choices allow you to discover if the student's preferences over a one-week all-expenses-paid vacation for two in (1) London, (2) Aspen, and (3) Honolulu are transitive. The other ten binary choices are window dressing--they are included so that the student doesn't immediately recognize his/her expressed intransitivities or the purpose of the experiment.

In reporting results, it is instructive to note that of the 27 possible responses to binary choices 1, 7, and 12, 13 are consistent with the transitivity assumption and 14 are not. The probability that a random response is consistent with transitivity is therefore about 1/2.

Copyright © 1991 W. H. Freeman and Company. All rights reserved.

Name: _____

INSTRUCTIONS
Experiment 4
Chapter 3 of <u>Microeconomics</u> by Eaton and Eaton

This experiment is designed to explore your preferences for vacation spots. In each of the 12 comparisons below, you are asked to consider a one-week all-expenses-paid vacation for two in two different destinations, labeled by A and B. If you prefer destination A, circle the "A" in the left margin. If you prefer destination B, circle the "B" in the left margin. If you are indifferent between the two destinations, circle the "I" in the left margin.

1. A B I (A) London, England
         (B) Aspen, Colorado

2. A B I (A) Palm Springs, California
         (B) Fort Lauderdale, Florida

3. A B I (A) Honolulu, Hawaii
         (B) New York City

4. A B I (A) Tokyo
         (B) New Orleans, Louisiana

5. A B I (A) Vancouver, Canada
         (B) Sydney, Australia

6. A B I (A) Tokyo
         (B) New York City

7. A B I (A) Aspen, Colorado
         (B) Honolulu, Hawaii

8. A B I (A) St. Moritz, Switzerland
         (B) Vancouver, Canada

9. A B I (A) Sydney, Australia
         (B) London, England

10. A B I (A) Fort Lauderdale, Florida
          (B) St. Moritz, Switzerland

11. A B I (A) New Orleans, Louisiana
          (B) Fort Lauderdale, Florida

12. A B I (A) London, England
          (B) Honolulu, Hawaii

Copyright © 1991 W. H. Freeman and Company. All rights reserved.

NOTE TO THE INSTRUCTOR
Experiment 5
Chapter 6 of *Microeconomics* by Eaton and Eaton

This experiment, which is designed to give students some idea of the extent to which preferences over risky prospects are consistent with expected utility theory, is for use in conjunction with Chapter 6. It takes about 15 minutes of class time to perform the experiment and about 30 minutes to tabulate results for a class of 50 students. We recommend that you perform the experiment just before your first lecture on Chapter 6 and that you discuss the results immediately after your discussion of the expected utility theorem.

Students are asked to construct their preference orderings over four risky prospects involving the prizes $10,000, $6,000, and $1,000. There are 49 possible preference orderings. Eleven are consistent with the theory and 38 are not. The eleven consistent preference orderings are

	(1)	(2)	(3)	(4)	(5)	(6)	(7)	(8)	(9)	(10)	(11)
First Choice	A	A,D	D	D	D	D,B	B	B	B	B	B
Second Choice	D	B,C	A	A,B	B	A	D	D	D	C,D	C
Third Choice	C		B	C	A	C	A	A,C	C	A	D
Fourth Choice	B		C		C		C		A		A

The simplest way to verify these results is to construct an expected utility function with one free parameter. Let the utility associated with the $10,000 prize be 1 and the utility associated with the $1,000 prize be 0, and denote the utility associated with the $6,000 prize by the parameter b, which is larger than 0 and less than 1. The following table associates the 11 consistent preference orderings with the values of b which induce the ordering.

Preference Ordering	Values of B
1	(0, 1/2)
2	1/2
3	(1/2, 5/9)
4	5/9
5	(5/9, 4/7)
6	4/7
7	(4/7, 3/5)
8	3/5
9	(3/5, 2/3)
10	2/3
11	(2/3, 1)

Copyright © 1991 W. H. Freeman and Company. All rights reserved.

A value of b = 5/9 corresponds to risk-neutral preferences. The first three preference orderings therefore reflect risk-inclined preferences and the last seven reflect risk-averse preferences.

In commenting on the results, it is instructive to discuss in detail one of the consistent orderings and one of the inconsistent orderings, showing why the first is consistent and the second is not. You can use the expected utility function described above to determine whether any particular preference ordering is consistent. For example, consider the inconsistent ordering A, B, C, D. A preferred to B requires b < 5/9; B preferred to C required b > 1/2; C preferred to D requires b > 2/3. Since there is no value of b which satisfies all three inequalities, the ordering is not consistent with the theory of expected utility.

Name: _____

INSTRUCTIONS
Experiment 5
Chapter 6 of <u>Microeconomics</u> by Eaton and Eaton

Try to imagine yourself in the following fortunate situation. On your desk are four brown bags labeled A, B, C, and D, and in each bag are ten bills. Bag A contains five $10,000 bills and five $1,000 bills. Bag B contains nine $6,000 bills and one $1,000 bill. (Of course, there are no $6,000 bills, but you can imagine them.) Bag C contains two $10,000 bills, five $6,000 bills, and three $1,000 bills. Bag D contains four $10,000 bills, two $6,000 bills, and four $1,000 bills. The bags and their contents are tabulated below:

Bag A	Bag B	Bag C	Bag D
5 $10,000 bills	9 $6,000 bills	2 $10,000 bills	4 $10,000 bills
5 $1,000 bills	1 $1,000 bill	5 $6,000 bills	2 $6,000 bills
		3 $1,000 bills	4 $1,000 bills

The rules of the game are that you can choose a bag, put a blindfold on, and then pick one bill from the bag you chose. You get to keep that bill.

Below, we want you to rank these four bags. That is, assuming that you get to randomly pick one bill from one of the four bags, we want you to indicate which bag would be your first choice, which would be your second choice, and so on. If you are indifferent between two or more bags, put all of their letters on the same line.

_____ First Choice
_____ Second Choice
_____ Third Choice
_____ Fourth Choice

Copyright © 1991 W. H. Freeman and Company. All rights reserved.

NOTE TO THE INSTRUCTOR
Experiment 6
Chapter 6 of <u>Microeconomics</u> by Eaton and Eaton

This experiment is subversive in the sense that it is designed to generate evidence which is inconsistent with the hypothesis that people maximize expected utility. It takes about 10 minutes of class time to conduct the experiment and perhaps 15 minutes to tabulate results. Because the issues raised by the experiment are quite serious, you might want to spend an entire lecture discussing the results. We suggest that you introduce the experiment either before you being to lecture on risk or after you have completed your discussion of the expected utility theorem. In either case, you will want to discuss the results only after you have considered the theorem.

In a series of four binary choices, students are asked to indicate which prospect is preferred: A1 or B1, A2 or B2, A3 or B3, A4 or B4. The first pair of binary choices forms one experiment and the second forms another. Past experiments suggest that a large percentage of your students will pick A1 and B2 in the first experiment and A3 and B4 in the second experiment. These preferences are <u>not</u> consistent with the hypothesis that individuals maximize expected utility.

One insightful way of seeing that choosing A1 and B2 is inconsistent with the theory is this: Using our prospect notation, A1 is (0, 1, 0: 4000, 3000, 0), B1 is (.8, 0, .2: 4000, 3000,. 0), and A2 is (0, .25, .75: 4000, 3000, 0). Notice that prospect B2, (.20, 0, .80: 4000, 3000, 0), can be generated from A2 by substituting B1 for the $3000 prize in A2. Therefore if A1 is preferred to B1, then the theory predicts that A2 is preferred to B2; conversely, if B1 is preferred to A1, then B2 should be preferred A2. Similarly, the theory predicts that if A3 is preferred to B3, then A4 is preferred to B4; conversely, if B3 is preferred to A3, then B4 should be preferred to A4.

For a thoughtful discussion of the issues raised by this sort of evidence and possible responses to the evidence, see Mark Machina, "Choice Under Uncertainty: Problems Solved and Unsolved," <u>Journal of Economic Perspectives</u>, Summer 1987, pp. 121-154.

Name: _____

INSTRUCTIONS
Experiment 6
Chapter 6 of *Microeconomics* by Eaton and Eaton

This experiment is designed to explore some aspects of your preferences in situations involving risk. In each of the four comparisons below we want you to indicate the prospect that you prefer by circling the appropriate letter in the left-hand margin. For example, in comparison 1 circle A1 if you prefer Prospect A1 to Prospect B1, circle B1 if you prefer Prospect B1 to Prospect A1, and circle I if you are indifferent between them.

1. A1 B1 I   Prospect A1: 100% chance of $3,000
                       Prospect B1:   80% chance of $4,000

2. A2 B2 I   Prospect A2:   25% chance of $3,000
                       Prospect B2:   20% chance of $4,000

3. A3 B3 I   Prospect A3:   95% chance of $6,000
                       Prospect B3:   75% chance of $8,000

4. A4 B4 I   Prospect A4:   19% chance of $6,000
                       Prospect B4:   15% chance of $8,000

Copyright © 1991 W. H. Freeman and Company. All rights reserved.

NOTE TO THE INSTRUCTOR
Experiments 7 and 8
Chapter 10 of <u>Microeconomics</u> by Eaton and Eaton

Both Experiments 7 and 8 are designed to give students some idea of the accuracy of the predictions of the competitive model. You can use either or both of them. They are similar to the experiments briefly discussed in Chapter 10. It takes from 15 to 25 minutes of class time to perform each experiment, depending on the number of students you include in the experiment, and up to 30 minutes to tabulate results.

Experiment 7 employs a casual trading mechanism: students simply circulate around the classroom trying to strike a deal. Experiment 8 employs a double-oral-auction trading mechanism.

To implement Experiment 7, you first need to choose one of the five variants described in Table 1. The entries in the body of the table are the numbers of students who are assigned various reservation prices. For example, for an experiment involving 20 students, assign 3 students a reservation demand price (RD) of $300, 1 student a reservation supply price (RS) of $290, 2 students an RD of $280, 2 students an RS of $270, and so on. Having chosen an experiment, make the required number of copies of the Buyer's (Seller's) Instruction Sheet for Experiment 7 and then fill in the blanks marked "reference demand price" and "reference supply price" on the instruction sheets to replicate the chosen experiment. Attach a paper clip to each copy of the Seller's Instruction Sheet. (The "magic" paper clip is the object of trade and is used to keep track of transactions.) Give students about five minutes to read and think about the instructions. Before allowing them to circulate, explain the instructions and ask for questions. You will need to announce the length of the trading period and to appoint someone to act as a timekeeper.

To implement Experiment 8, first choose one of the five variants described in Table 2. Notice that these variants are identical to those in Table 1 with one exception--all reservation prices are $80 higher. Thus, if you choose to conduct both experiments, experience in the first one does not "spoil" the second one. Make the required number of copies of the Buyer's (Seller's) Instruction Sheet and fill in the blanks as in Experiment 7. (Notice that these instructions sheets cover two pages.) Attach a paper clip to each copy of the Seller's Instruction Sheet. Give students at least five minutes to read the instructions. Since the instructions are long and somewhat complex, you <u>must</u> explain them in detail and ask for questions before you conduct the experiment. Appoint an auctioneer, a secretary of trading, and a timekeeper. If you choose to include a large number of students in the experiment, you'll need two or three secretaries.

Copyright © 1991 W. H. Freeman and Company. All rights reserved.

There are a number of interesting variations on these experiments, two of which are easily implemented using our instruction sheets. First, you are obviously not limited to the experiments (demand and supply functions) described in Tables 1 and 2. You can devise your own experiment and use our instruction sheets to implement it. If you do, we would be interested in seeing the results but cannot promise to circulate them to other instructors.

Second, you can get students to reveal their own reservation prices for some real good—for example, a ticket to the first game of the World Series. Give half the students the Buyer's Instruction Sheet and half the Seller's Instruction Sheet with a paper clip attached. Instead of assigning reservation prices to your students, ask them to write down their own reservation prices for the real good that you choose and to think of the paper clip as a unit of the good. Then conduct the experiment. Again, we would like to see results but can't promise to circulate them.

TABLE 1
Chapter 10, Experiment 7
$250 < p^e < $260

		n=20 $y^e=7$ T=5		n=40 $y^e=15$ T=8		n=60 $y^e=24$ T=10		n=80 $y^e=30$ T=12		n=100 $y^e=40$ T=15	
RD	RS	RD	RS	RD	RS	RD	RS	RD	RS	RD	RS
$300	–	3	–	5	–	8	–	10	–	10	–
–	$290	–	1	–	2	–	2	–	5	–	5
$280	–	2	–	5	–	8	–	10	–	20	–
–	$270	–	2	–	3	–	4	–	5	–	5
$260	–	2	–	5	–	8	–	10	–	10	–
–	$250	–	2	–	5	–	8	–	10	–	10
$240	–	2	–	3	–	4	–	5	–	5	–
–	$230	–	2	–	5	–	8	–	10	–	20
$220	–	1	–	2	–	2	–	5	–	5	–
–	$210	–	3	–	5	–	8	–	10	–	10

Table 2
Chapter 10, Experiment 2
$330 < p^e < $340

		n=20 $y^e=7$ T=5		n=40 $y^e=15$ T=8		n=60 $y^e=24$ T=10		n=80 $y^e=30$ T=12		n=100 $y^e=40$ T=15	
RD	RS	RD	RS	RD	RS	RD	RS	RD	RS	RD	RS
$380	–	3	–	5	–	8	–	10	–	10	–
–	$370	–	1	–	2	–	2	–	5	–	5
$360	–	2	–	5	–	8	–	10	–	20	–
–	$350	–	2	–	3	–	4	–	5	–	5
$340	–	2	–	5	–	8	–	10	–	10	–
–	$330	–	2	–	5	–	8	–	10	–	10
$320	–	2	–	3	–	4	–	5	–	5	–
–	$310	–	2	–	5	–	8	–	10	–	20
$300	–	1	–	2	–	2	–	5	–	5	–
–	$290	–	3	–	5	–	8	–	10	–	10

n = number of students
p^e = equilibrium price
y^e = equilibrium quantity
T = suggested trading time in minutes

Copyright © 1991 W. H. Freeman and Company. All rights reserved.

Name: _____

BUYER'S INSTRUCTION SHEET
Experiment 7
Chapter 10 of <u>Microeconomics</u> by Eaton and Eaton

After you have read these instructions, you will be given the opportunity to try to negotiate the purchase of a "magic" paper clip from one of your classmates. Students with paper clips on their instruction sheets will be trying to sell their paper clips, and students without paper clips will be trying to buy one.

You've been given what we will call a <u>reference demand price</u>. It is **reference demand price = $ _____ .**

You are to <u>imagine</u> the following:

(i) If you negotiate a deal to buy a paper clip for a price that is <u>smaller</u> <u>than</u> your reference price, your instructor will give you the difference between your reference price and the negotiated price.

(ii) If you negotiate a deal for a price that is <u>larger</u> <u>than</u> your reference price, you will have to pay your instructor the difference between the negotiated price and your reference price.

(iii) You may be unable to negotiate a deal that is acceptable to you. If you do not strike a deal, you will not get any money nor will you lose any.

In other words, imagine that you will get real money if you buy at a price less than your reference price and that you will lose real money if you buy at a price larger than your reference price.

When the instructor announces that "the market is open," you can circulate throughout the room trying to strike a deal. If you do strike a deal, write down the negotiated price at the bottom of this instruction sheet and at the bottom of the seller's instruction sheet. Then use your magic paper clip to clip the two sheets together and return them to your instructor.

Negotiated Price $ _____ .

Copyright © 1991 W. H. Freeman and Company. All rights reserved.

Name: _____

SELLER'S INSTRUCTION SHEET
Experiment 7
Chapter 10 of <u>Microeconomics</u> by Eaton and Eaton

After you have read these instructions, you will be given the opportunity to try to negotiate the sale of the "magic" paper clip attached to this instruction sheet to one of your classmates. Students with paper clips on their instruction sheets will be trying to sell the paper clips, and students without paper clips will be trying to buy one.

You have been given what we will call a <u>reference supply price</u>. It is **reference supply price = $ _____** .

You are to <u>imagine</u> the following:

(i) If you negotiate a deal to sell the paper clip for a price that is <u>larger than</u> your reference price, your instructor will give you the difference between the negotiated price and your reference price.

(ii) If you negotiate a deal for a price that is <u>less than</u> your reference price, you will have to pay your instructor the difference between your reference price and the negotiated price.

(iii) You may be unable to negotiate a deal which is acceptable to you. If you do not strike a deal, you will not get any money nor will you lose any.

In other words, imagine that you will get real money if you sell at a price larger than your reference price, and that you will lose real money if you sell at a price smaller than your reference price.

When the instructor announces that "the market is open," you can circulate throughout the room trying to strike a deal. If you do strike a deal, write down the negotiated price at the bottom of this instruction sheet and at the bottom of the buyer's instructions sheet. Then use the magic paper clip to clip the two sheets together and return them to your instructor.

Negotiated Price $ _____ .

Copyright © 1991 W. H. Freeman and Company. All rights reserved.

Name: _____

BUYER'S INSTRUCTION SHEET
Experiment 8
Chapter 10 of <u>Microeconomics</u> by Eaton and Eaton

After you have read these instructions, you will be given a chance to buy a "magic" paper clip from one of your classmates. Students with paper clips on their instruction sheets will be trying to sell their paper clips and students without paper clips will be trying to buy one.

You have been given what we will call a <u>reference demand price</u>. It is **reference demand price = $ _____**.

You are to <u>imagine</u> the following:

(i) If you buy a paper clip for a price that is <u>smaller than</u> your reference price, your instructor will give you the difference between your reference price and the negotiated price.

(ii) If you buy a paper clip for a price that is <u>larger than</u> your reference price, you will have to give your instructor the difference between the negotiated price and your reference price.

(iii) If you do not buy a paper clip, you will get nothing from the instructor nor will you have to give the instructor anything.

In other words, imagine that you will get real money if you buy at a price less than your reference price and that you will lose real money if you buy at a price larger than your reference price.

In addition to the buyers and sellers, the experiment also involves an "auctioneer" who will post "bid" and "ask prices," a "secretary of trading" who will record transactions, and a "timekeeper" who will close the market when a specified period of time has elapsed. When the auctioneer announces that "the market is open," he or she will begin by asking for a "bid price" from a buyer and an "ask price" from a seller and will then post both prices on the blackboard. Of course, you are free to announce a "bid price" if no one else announces one first. A buyer's "bid price" is a price that the buyer is willing to pay and a seller's "ask price" is a price that the seller is willing to accept.

Copyright © 1991 W. H. Freeman and Company. All rights reserved.

Whenever a "bid price" and an "ask price" are posted on the blackboard, you have the following options:

(i) You can accept the posted "bid price." If you do accept it, you and the buyer who announced the posted "bid price" must take your instruction sheets to the trading desk. The secretary of trading will then record the price at which you sold the paper clip at the bottom of this page and at the bottom of the buyer's instruction sheet and, using the magic paper clip, will clip the instruction sheets together. In the meantime, the auctioneer will solicit a new "bid price" from some other buyer, posting it on the blackboard.

(ii) You can announce an "ask price" which is <u>lower than</u> the posted "ask price." If you do, the auctioneer will erase the posted "ask price" and post the one you announced.

Buyers have similar options:

(i) Any buyer can accept the posted "ask price." If one does, the buyer and the seller who announced the posted "ask price" must take their instruction sheets to the trading desk where the secretary will record the transaction and clip the instruction sheets together. In the meantime, the auctioneer will solicit a new "ask price."

(ii) Any buyer can announce a "bid price" which is <u>higher than</u> the posted "bid price." If one does, the auctioneer will erase the posted "bid price" and post the higher one announced by the buyer.

Once all buyers and sellers have read their instruction sheets and have understood the trading rule, the auctioneer will announce the length of the trading period and declare that "the market is open." Every ten seconds thereafter the timekeeper will write the time remaining in the trading period on the blackboard. When the time expires, the timekeeper will announce that "the market is closed," and no further transactions can be made.

Transaction Price _____

Copyright © 1991 W. H. Freeman and Company. All rights reserved.

Name: _____

SELLER'S INSTRUCTION SHEET
Experiment Number 8
Chapter 10 of <u>Microeconomics</u> by Eaton and Eaton

After you have read these instructions, you will be given a chance to sell the "magic" paper clip attached to this instruction sheet to one of your classmates. Students with paper clips on their instruction sheets will be trying to sell their paper clips, and students without paper clips will be trying to buy one.

You have been given what we will call a <u>reference supply price</u>. It is **reference supply price = $_____**.

You are to <u>imagine</u> the following:

(i)   If you sell this paper clip for a price that is <u>larger than</u> your reference supply price, your instructor will give you the difference between the negotiated price and your reference price.

(ii) If you sell for a price which is <u>less than</u> your reference price, you will have to pay your instructor the difference between your reference price and the negotiated price.

(iii) You may be unable to sell the paper clip at a price acceptable to you. If you do not sell it, you will not get any money nor will you lose any.

In other words, imagine that you will get real money if you sell at a price larger than your reference price and that you will lose real money if you sell at a price less than your reference price.

In addition to buyers and sellers, the experiment also involves an "auctioneer" who will post "bid" and "ask prices," a "secretary of trading" who will record transactions, and a "timekeeper" who will close the market when a specified period of time has elapsed. When the auctioneer announces that "the market is open," he or she will begin by asking for a "bid price" from a buyer and an "ask price" from a seller, and will then post both prices on the blackboard. Of course, you are free to announce an "ask price" if no one else announces one first. A buyer's "bid price" is a price that the buyer is willing to pay, and a seller's "ask price" is a price that the seller is willing to accept.

Copyright © 1991 W. H. Freeman and Company. All rights reserved.

Whenever a "bid price" and an "ask price" are posted on the blackboard, you have the following options":

(i) You can accept the posted "ask price." If you do accept it, both you and the seller who announced the posted "ask price" must take your instruction sheets to the trading desk. The secretary of trading will then record the price at which you bought the paper clip on your instruction sheet and on the seller's instruction sheet and, using the magic paper clip, will clip the instruction sheets together. In the meantime, the auctioneer will solicit a new "ask price" from some other seller, posting it on the blackboard.

(ii) You can announce a "bid price" which is higher than the posted "bid price." If you do, the auctioneer will erase the posted "bid price" and post the one you announced.

Sellers have similar options:

(i) Any seller can accept the posted "bid price." If one does, the seller and the buyer who announced the posted "bid price" must take their instruction sheets to the trading desk where the secretary will record the transaction and clip the instruction sheets together. In the meantime, the auctioneer will solicit a new "bid price."

(ii) Any seller can announce an "ask price" which is lower than the posted "ask price." If one does, the auctioneer will erase the posted "ask price" and post the lower one announced by the seller.

Once all buyers and sellers have read their instruction sheets and have understood the trading rule, the auctioneer will announce the length of the trading period and declare that "the market is open." Every ten seconds thereafter the timekeeper will write the time remaining in the trading period on the blackboard. When the time expires, the timekeeper will announce that "the market is closed," and no further transactions can be made.

Transaction Price _____

Copyright © 1991 W. H. Freeman and Company. All rights reserved.

NOTE TO THE INSTRUCTOR
Experiment 9
Chapter 12 of _Microeconomics_ by Eaton and Eaton

This experiment, which involves four versions of the Prisoner's Dilemma game, is designed to be used in conjunction with Chapter 12. It takes about 10 minutes of class time to perform the experiment and about 15 minutes to tabulate results for a class of 50. We suggest that you conduct the experiment just before your first lecture on oligopoly and that you discuss the results just after you have lectured on the concept of Nash equilibrium.

The strategic (or normal) forms of the four games are presented below. Player B's strategies are across the top and Player A's are down the side of each matrix. In each cell of the matrix, A's payoff is listed first and B's is second.

	Game 1		Game 2		Game 3		Game 4	
	1	2	1	2	1	2	1	2
1	200/200	90/280	200/200	20/280	200/200	90/210	200/200	20/210
2	280/90	100/100	280/20	100/100	210/90	100/100	210/20	100/100

In each game the unique noncooperative equilibrium is (2,2). However, the incentives for either player to choose 2 over 1 are quite different in the four games.

The noncooperative equilibrium is most likely in Game 2; regardless of which strategy B chooses, the gain to A associated with choosing strategy 2 over 1 is $80. It is least likely in Game 3; regardless of which strategy B chooses, the gain to A from choosing strategy 2 over 1 is only $10. In Game 1 (Game 4), the gain to player A associated with choosing 2 over 1 is $80 ($10) if A anticipates that B will choose strategy 1, and it is $10 ($80) if A anticipates that B will choose 2. These variations in the incentives associated with noncooperative behavior are intended to give the student some notion of the circumstances in which the noncooperative equilibrium is and is not useful in predicting behavior.

To implement the experiment, make approximately n/4 copies of the instructions for each game, where n is the number of students in your course. Hand out the instructions and give the students five minutes to think about a choice of strategy. Because each student is instructed to imagine that he or she has never seen the other player, you do not need to form pairs of students.

Copyright © 1991 W. H. Freeman and Company. All rights reserved.

Name: _____

INSTRUCTIONS FOR GAME 1
Experiment 9
Chapter 12 of <u>Microeconomics</u> by Eaton and Eaton

Imagine yourself in the following game situation, involving two players--you and another player we will call B--and a host with lots of money. You and B are complete strangers and you are isolated in separate cubicles. The host gives each of you a card with your name on it, instructing each of you to write a 1 or a 2 on the card. The host then collects the cards and gives each player a sum of money determined by the numbers written on the cards. If both you and B write down a 1, then each of you gets $200. If both you and B write down a 2, then each of you gets $100. If one of you writes down a 1 and the other writes down a 2, then the player who writes down 1 gets $90 and the player who writes down 2 gets $280. The host's payoff rules are summarized in the following table:

B's number	Your Number	Your Payoff	B's Payoff
1	1	$200	$200
1	2	$280	$ 90
2	1	$ 90	$280
2	2	$100	$100

The first line of the table corresponds to the case in which both you and B write down a 1, the second to the case in which B writes down and 1 and you write down a 2, the third to the case in which B writes down a 2 and you write down a 1, and the fourth to the case in which both you and B write down a 2.

Before you indicate what number you would choose consider the following questions: What pair of numbers yields the largest total payoff? What pair yields the smallest total payoff? If you were sure that B would choose 1, what number would you choose? If you were sure that B would choose 2, what number would you choose?

Put an X beside the number that you would write on your card.

_____ 1

_____ 2

Copyright © 1991 W. H. Freeman and Company. All rights reserved.

Name: _____

INSTRUCTIONS FOR GAME 2
Experiment 9
Chapter 12 of <u>Microeconomics</u> by Eaton and Eaton

Imagine yourself in the following game situation, involving two players--you and another player we will call B--and a host with lots of money. You and B are complete strangers and you are isolated in separate cubicles. The host gives each of you a card with your name on it, instructing each of you to write a 1 or a 2 on the card. The host then collects the cards and gives each player a sum of money determined by the numbers written on the cards. If both you and B write down a 1, then each of you gets $200. If both you and B write down a 2, then each of you gets $100. If one of you writes down a 1 and the other writes down a 2, then the player who writes down 1 gets $20 and the player who writes down 2 gets $280. The host's payoff rules are summarized in the following table:

B's number	Your Number	Your Payoff	B's Payoff
1	1	$200	$200
1	2	$280	$20
2	1	$20	$280
2	2	$100	$100

The first line of the table corresponds to the case in which both you and B write down a 1, the second to the case in which B writes down and 1 and you write down a 2, the third to the case in which B writes down a 2 and you write down a 1, and the fourth to the case in which both you and B write down a 2.

Before you indicate what number you would choose consider the following questions: What pair of numbers yields the largest total payoff? What pair yields the smallest total payoff? If you were sure that B would choose 1, what number would you choose? If you were sure that B would choose 2, what number would you choose?

Put an X beside the number that you would write on your card.

_____ 1

_____ 2

Copyright © 1991 W. H. Freeman and Company. All rights reserved.

Report the results separately for each of the four games. For each game report the number of students who chose strategies 1 and 2 as well as the expected payoffs associated with each strategy. For example, let n_1 and n_2 denote the numbers of players who chose 1 and 2 in Game 1. The expected payoff to a player who chose strategy 1 is then

$$\$200[(n_1 - 1)/(n_1 + n_2 - 1)] + \$90[n_2/(n_1 + n_2 - 1)],$$

and the expected payoff to a player who chose strategy 2 is

$$\$280[n_1/(n_1 + n_2 - 1)] + \$100[(n_2 - 1)/(n_1 + n_2 - 1)].$$

Name: _____

INSTRUCTIONS FOR GAME 3
Experiment 9
Chapter 12 of <u>Microeconomics</u> by Eaton and Eaton

Imagine yourself in the following game situation, involving two players--you and another player we will call B--and a host with lots of money. You and B are complete strangers and you are isolated in separate cubicles. The host gives each of you a card with your name on it, instructing each of you to write a 1 or a 2 on the card. The host then collects the cards and gives each player a sum of money determined by the numbers written on the cards. If both you and B write down a 1, then each of you gets $200. If both you and B write down a 2, then each of you gets $100. If one of you writes down a 1 and the other writes down a 2, then the player who writes down 1 gets $90 and the player who writes down 2 gets $210. The host's payoff rules are summarized in the following table:

B's number	Your Number	Your Payoff	B's Payoff
1	1	$200	$200
1	2	$210	$ 90
2	1	$ 90	$210
2	2	$100	$100

The first line of the table corresponds to the case in which both you and B write down a 1, the second to the case in which B writes down and 1 and you write down a 2, the third to the case in which B writes down a 2 and you write down a 1, and the fourth to the case in which both you and B write down a 2.

Before you indicate what number you would choose consider the following questions: What pair of numbers yields the largest total payoff? What pair yields the smallest total payoff? If you were sure that B would choose 1, what number would you choose? If you were sure that B would choose 2, what number would you choose?

Put an X beside the number that you would write on your card.

_____ 1

_____ 2

Copyright © 1991 W. H. Freeman and Company. All rights reserved.

Name: _____

INSTRUCTIONS FOR GAME 4
Experiment 9
Chapter 12 of <u>Microeconomics</u> by Eaton and Eaton

Imagine yourself in the following game situation, involving two players—you and another player we will call B—and a host with lots of money. You and B are complete strangers and you are isolated in separate cubicles. The host gives each of you a card with your name on it, instructing each of you to write a 1 or a 2 on the card. The host then collects the cards and gives each player a sum of money determined by the numbers written on the cards. If both you and B write down a 1, then each of you gets $200. If both you and B write down a 2, then each of you gets $100. If one of you writes down a 1 and the other writes down a 2, then the player who writes down 1 gets $20 and the player who writes down 2 gets $210. The host's payoff rules are summarized in the following table:

B's number	Your Number	Your Payoff	B's Payoff
1	1	$200	$200
1	2	$210	$ 20
2	1	$ 20	$210
2	2	$100	$100

The first line of the table corresponds to the case in which both you and B write down a 1, the second to the case in which B writes down and 1 and you write down a 2, the third to the case in which B writes down a 2 and you write down a 1, and the fourth to the case in which both you and B write down a 2.

Before you indicate what number you would choose consider the following questions: What pair of numbers yields the largest total payoff? What pair yields the smallest total payoff? If you were sure that B would choose 1, what number would you choose? If you were sure that B would choose 2, what number would you choose?

Put an X beside the number that you would write on your card.

_____ 1

_____ 2

Copyright © 1991 W. H. Freeman and Company. All rights reserved.

NOTE TO THE INSTRUCTOR
Experiment 10
Chapter 17 of Microeconomics by Eaton and Eaton

A fundamental hypothesis in the property rights approach to externalities is that individuals, if given the opportunity, will negotiate Pareto-optimal solutions to externality problems. This experiment is designed to test this hypothesis and is inspired by Elizabeth Hoffman and Mathew Spitzer, "The Coase Theorem: Some Experimental Tests," Journal of Law and Economics, April 1982, pp. 73-98. It takes about 20 minutes of class time to run the experiment and perhaps 20 minutes to tabulate results for a class of 50. We suggest that you conduct the experiment before your first lecture on externalities and discuss results after you have lectured on the property rights approach.

The experiment involves 2 players, one of whom is (randomly) given the right to pick an integer: 1, 2, or 3. The integer in turn determines a payoff to both players. The payoffs are structured so that the integer that maximizes the private payoff to the player who gets to choose is either a 1 or a 3, whereas the sum of payoffs is maximized when a 2 is chosen. Before the integer is chosen, the 2 players are given the chance to negotiate a contract that specifies the integer to be chosen and a side payment from one player to the other. Of course, the hypothesis is that the players will agree to choose the integer 2 and that the side payment will be such that both players are better off than they would be in the absence of an agreement.

To implement the experiment, group students into pairs and give half of the pairs instructions for Version 1 of the experiment and the other half instructions for Version 2. Attach a paper clip to each instruction sheet for Player A. Give students five minutes to read the instructions and then explain them and ask for questions. Then toss a coin, write the result ("head" or "tail") on the board, and give students five minutes to negotiate a contract. The two versions of the experiment are designed so that Player A will have the right to choose the number in half of the pairs, and Player B will have the right to choose it in the other half. In all other respects, the two versions are identical.

Discuss the results for the two versions seperately. For each version, first identify the number of cases in which 2 was and and was not chosen, and for the cases in which 2 was chosen, identify the average magnitude of the side payment. When B has the right to choose, the side payment from A to B must be no smaller than $30 and no larger than $80 for the agreement to be Pareto-optimal relative to the default option in which B chooses 1. When A has the right to choose, Pareto optimality requires that the side payment form B to A must be no smaller than $40 and no larger than $140.

Copyright © 1991 W. H. Freeman and Company. All rights reserved.

Name: _____

INSTRUCTIONS FOR PLAYER A, VERSION 1
Experiment 10
Chapter 17 of <u>Microeconomics</u> by Eaton and Eaton

This game involves two players, A and B, and you are Player A. One of you will be given the opportunity to pick number 1, 2, or 3, and then we want you to imagine that your instructor will pay you a sum of money determined by the following table:

Number	A's Payoff	B's Payoff
1	$ 20	$180
2	$100	$150
3	$140	$ 10

If number 1 is picked you'll get $20 and B will get $180; if 2 is picked you'll get $100 and B will get $150; if 3 is picked you'll get $140 and B will get $10.

The lucky person who gets to pick the number will be determined by the flip of a coin. Your instructor will flip the coin and write the result on the blackboard. A head means that you get to pick the number and a tail means that B gets to pick the number.

After your instructor has flipped the coin but before the winner of the coin toss picks the number, the two of you will have five minutes to attempt to devise a contract specifying the number to be chosen and possible payments from one of you to the other. The contract form is reproduced below. On line 1 you must specify the chosen number and on line 2 you must indicate who pays what to whom.

For example, suppose that the two of you agreed to pick number 1 and that B should pay A $50. On line 1 you would put a "1" in the blank. On line 2 you would cross out the first A and the second B, and put "50" in the blank. This contract means that because "1" was chosen the instructor will pay you $20 and B $180 and then B will pay you $50.

(1) The chosen number is _____.

(2) Player   A   B   agrees to pay Player   A   B $ _____.

If you do not agree on some contract, then the player who has the right to pick the number should fill out the following:

The chosen number is _____.

Player B's instruction sheet has the same forms on it. After you've reached a decision, complete the appropriate form on both sheets, clip them together, and return them to your instructor.

Copyright © 1991 W. H. Freeman and Company. All rights reserved.

Name: _____

INSTRUCTIONS FOR PLAYER B, VERSION 1
Experiment 10
Chapter 17 of *Microeconomics* by Eaton and Eaton

This game involves two players, A and B, and you are Player B. One of you will be given the opportunity to pick number 1, 2, or 3, and then we want you to imagine that your instructor will pay you a sum of money determined by the following table:

Number	A's Payoff	B's Payoff
1	$ 20	$180
2	$100	$150
3	$140	$ 10

If number 1 is picked you'll get $180 and A will get $20; if 2 is picked you'll get $150 and A will get $100; if 3 is picked you'll get $10 and A will get $140.

The lucky person who gets to pick the number will be determined by the flip of a coin. Your instructor will flip the coin and write the result on the blackboard. A head means that A gets to pick the number and a tail means that you get to pick the number.

After your instructor has flipped the coin but before the winner of the coin toss picks the number, the two of you will have five minutes to attempt to devise a contract specifying the number to be chosen and possible payments from one of you to the other. The contract form is reproduced below. On line 1 you must specify the chosen number and on line 2 you must indicate who pays what to whom.

For example, suppose that the two of you agreed to pick number 1 and that B should pay A $50. On line 1 you would put a "1" in the blank. On line 2 you would cross out the first A and the second B, and put "50" in the blank. This contract means that because "1" was chosen the instructor will pay you $180 and A $20 and then you will pay A $50.

(1) The chosen number is _____.

(2) Player A B agrees to pay Player A B $ _____.

If you do not agree on some contract, then the player who has the right to pick the number should fill out the following:

The chosen number is _____.

Player A's instruction sheet has the same forms on it. After you've reached a decision, complete the appropriate form on both sheets, clip them together, and return them to your instructor.

Copyright © 1991 W. H. Freeman and Company. All rights reserved.

Name: _____

INSTRUCTIONS FOR PLAYER A, VERSION 2
Experiment 10
Chapter 17 of <u>Microeconomics</u> by Eaton and Eaton

This game involves two players, A and B, and you are Player A. One of you will be given the opportunity to pick number 1, 2, or 3, and then we want you to imagine that your instructor will pay you a sum of money determined by the following table:

Number	A's Payoff	B's Payoff
1	$20	$180
2	$100	$150
3	$140	$10

If number 1 is picked you'll get $20 and B will get $180; if 2 is picked you'll get $100 and B will get $150; if 3 is picked you'll get $140 and B will get $10.

The lucky person who gets to pick the number will be determined by the flip of a coin. Your instructor will flip the coin and write the result on the blackboard. A tail means that you get to pick the number and a head means that B gets to pick the number.

After your instructor has flipped the coin but before the winner of the coin toss picks the number, the two of you will have five minutes to attempt to devise a contract specifying the number to be chosen and possible payments from one of you to the other. The contract form is reproduced below. On line 1 you must specify the chosen number and on line 2 you must indicate who pays what to whom.

For example, suppose that the two of you agreed to pick number 1 and that B should pay A $50. On line 1 you would put a "1" in the blank. On line 2 you would cross out the first A and the second B, and put "50" in the blank. This contract means that because "1" was chosen the instructor will pay you $20 and B $180 and then B will pay you $50.

(1) The chosen number is _____.

(2) Player   A   B   agrees to pay Player   A   B $ _____.

If you do not agree on some contract, then the player who has the right to pick the number should fill out the following:

The chosen number is _____.

Player B's instruction sheet has the same forms on it. After you've reached a decision, complete the appropriate form on both sheets, clip them together, and return them to your instructor.

Copyright © 1991 W. H. Freeman and Company. All rights reserved.

Name: _____

INSTRUCTIONS FOR PLAYER B, VERSION 2
Experiment 10
Chapter 17 of <u>Microeconomics</u> by Eaton and Eaton

This game involves two players, A and B, and you are Player B. One of you will be given the opportunity to pick number 1, 2, or 3, and then we want you to imagine that your instructor will pay you a sum of money determined by the following table:

Number	A's Payoff	B's Payoff
1	$ 20	$180
2	$100	$150
3	$140	$ 10

If number 1 is picked you'll get $180 and A will get $20; if 2 is picked you'll get $150 and A will get $100; if 3 is picked you'll get $10 and A will get $140.

The lucky person who gets to pick the number will be determined by the flip of a coin. Your instructor will flip the coin and write the result on the blackboard. A tail means that A gets to pick the number and a head means that you get to pick the number.

After your instructor has flipped the coin but before the winner of the coin toss picks the number, the two of you will have five minutes to attempt to devise a contract specifying the number to be chosen and possible payments from one of you to the other. The contract form is reproduced below. On line 1 you must specify the chosen number and on line 2 you must indicate who pays what to whom.

For example, suppose that the two of you agreed to pick number 1 and that B should pay A $50. On line 1 you would put a "1" in the blank. On line 2 you would cross out the first A and the second B, and put "50" in the blank. This contract means that because "1" was chosen the instructor will pay you $180 and A $20 and then you will pay A $50.

(1) The chosen number is _____.

(2) Player A B agrees to pay Player A B $ _____.

If you do not agree on some contract, then the player who has the right to pick the number should fill out the following:

The chosen number is _____.

Player A's instruction sheet has the same forms on it. After you've reached a decision, complete the appropriate form on both sheets, clip them together, and return them to your instructor.

Copyright © 1991 W. H. Freeman and Company. All rights reserved.

Transparency Masters

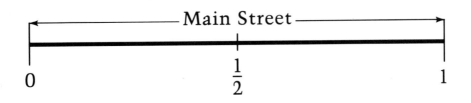

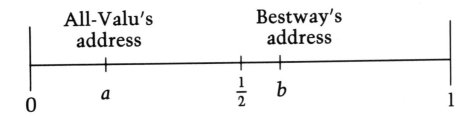

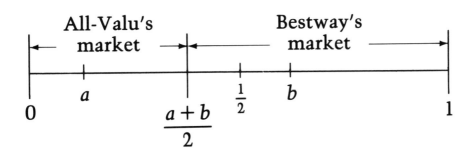

Figures 1.1, 1.2, 1.3

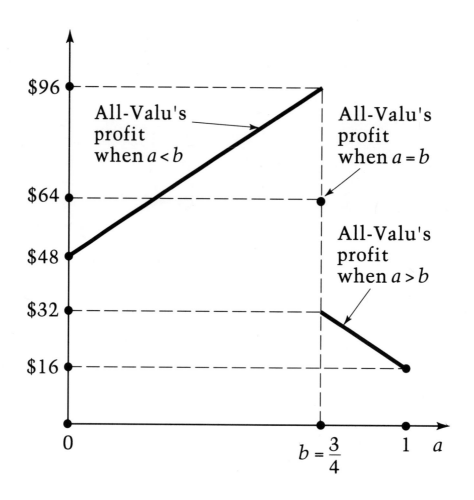

Figure 1.4

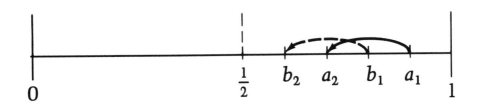

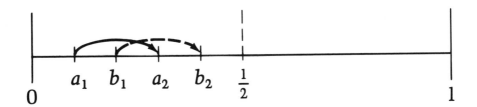

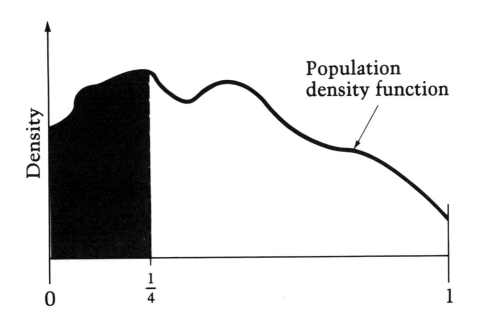

Figures 1.5, 1.6

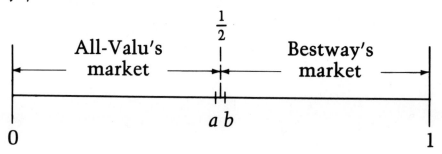

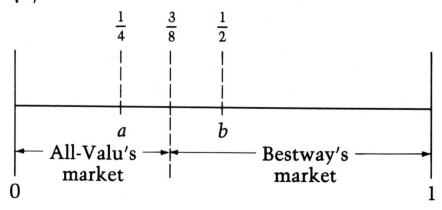

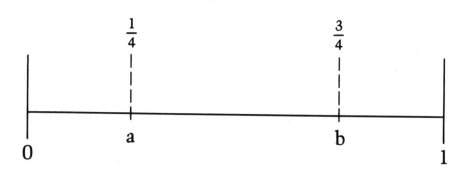

Figures 1.7, 1.8

Eaton and Eaton: MICROECONOMICS, Second Edition

© 1991, W. H. Freeman and Company

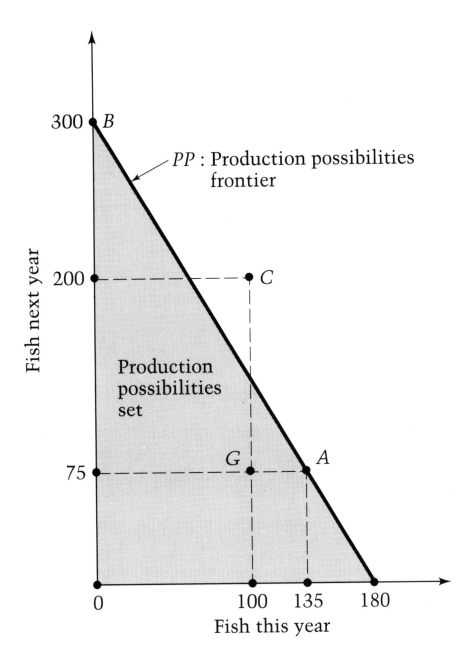

Figure 2.1

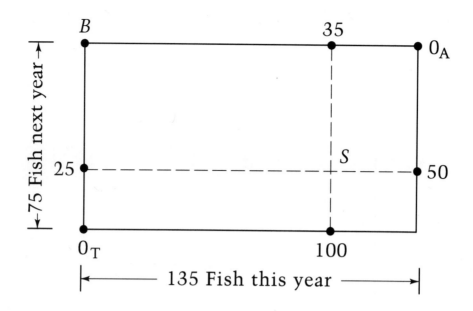

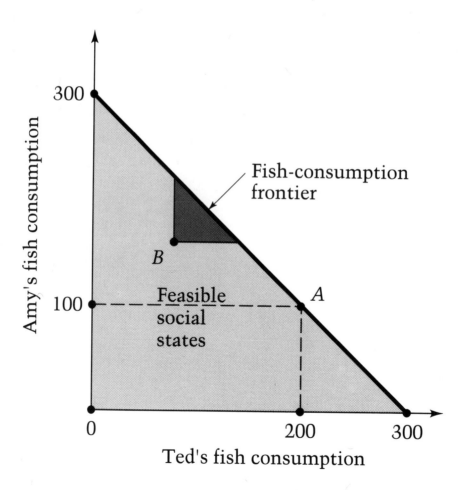

Figures 2.2, 2.3

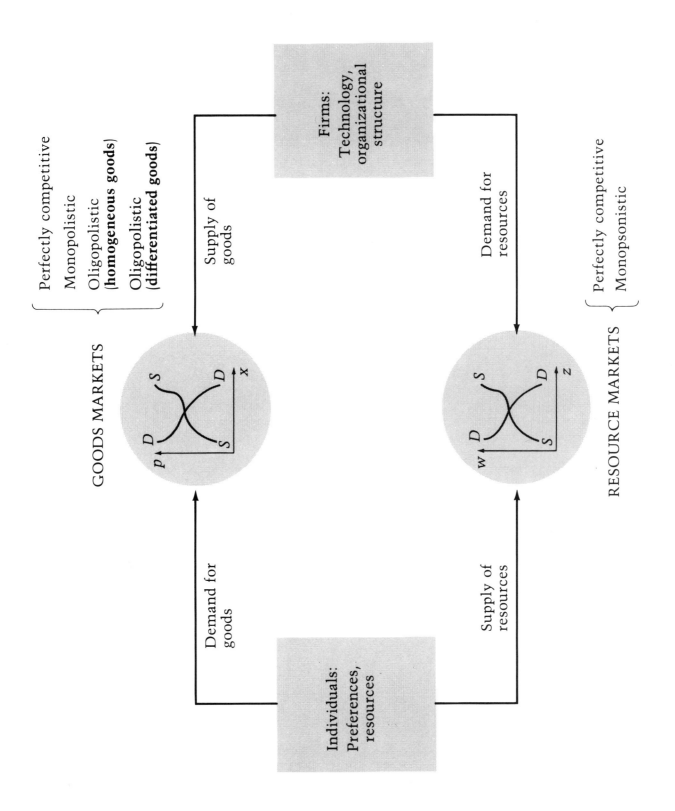

Figure 2.4

Eaton and Eaton: MICROECONOMICS, Second Edition

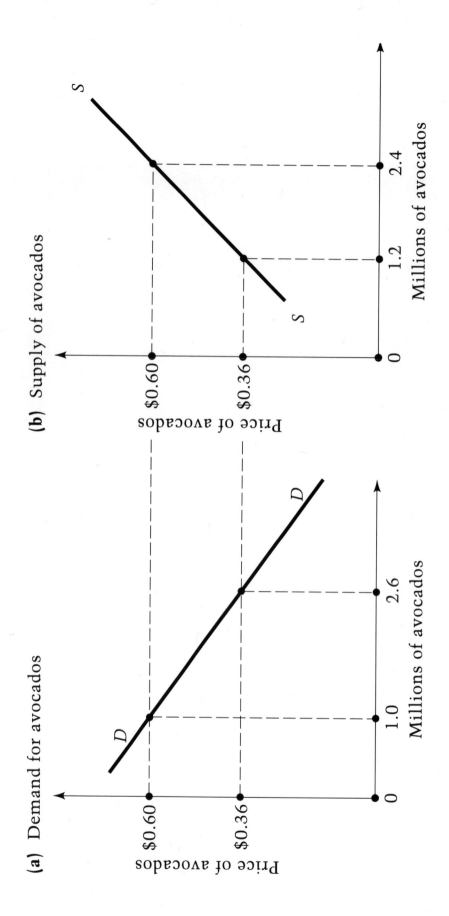

Figure 2.5

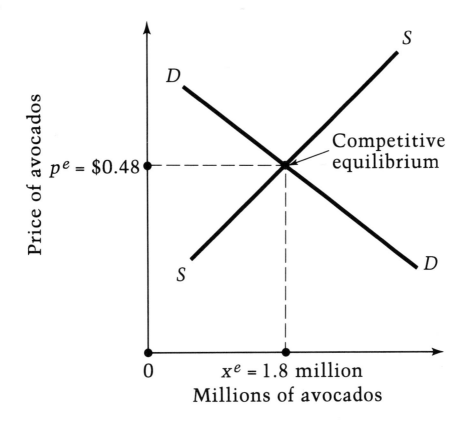
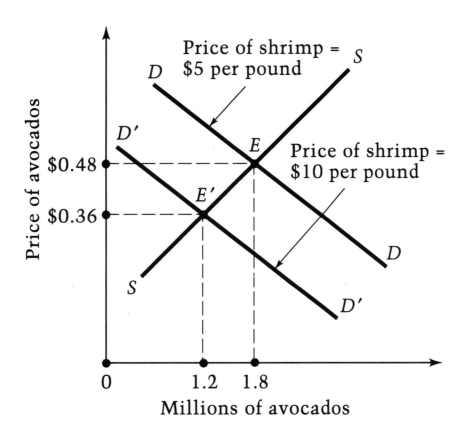

Figures 2.6, 2.7

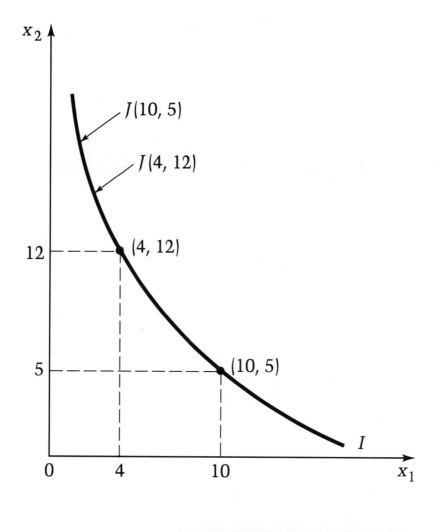

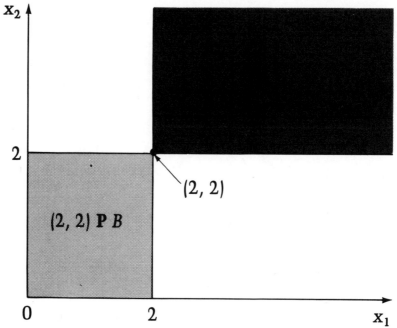

Figures 3.1, 3.2

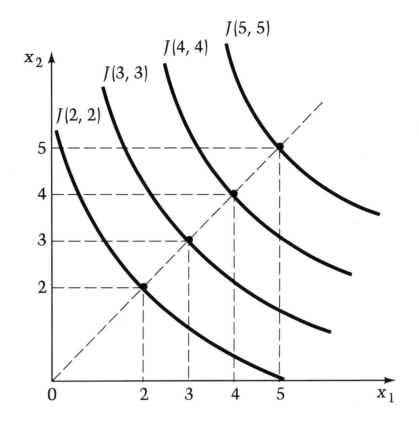

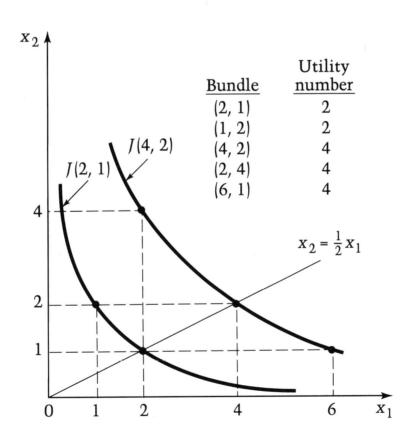

Figures 3.3, 3.4

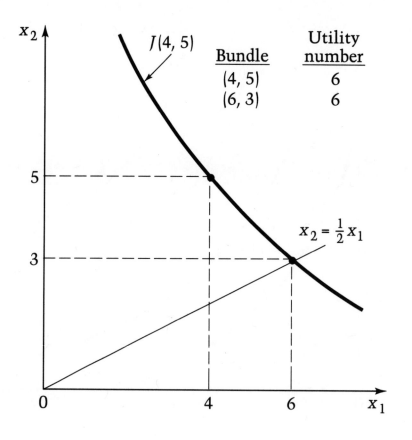

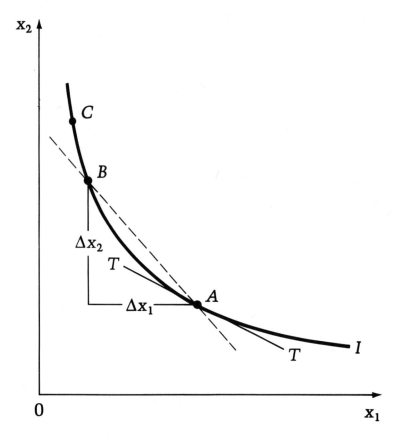

Figures 3.5, 3.6

Eaton and Eaton: MICROECONOMICS, Second Edition

© 1991, W. H. Freeman and Company

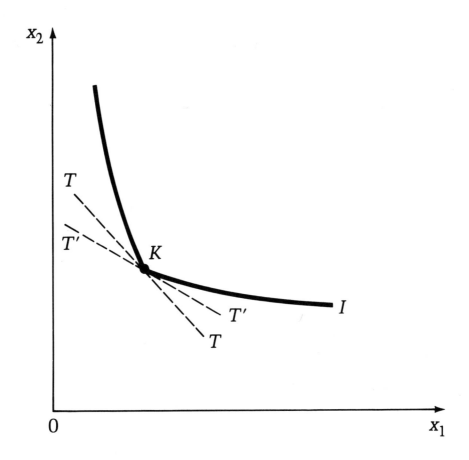

Figure 3.7

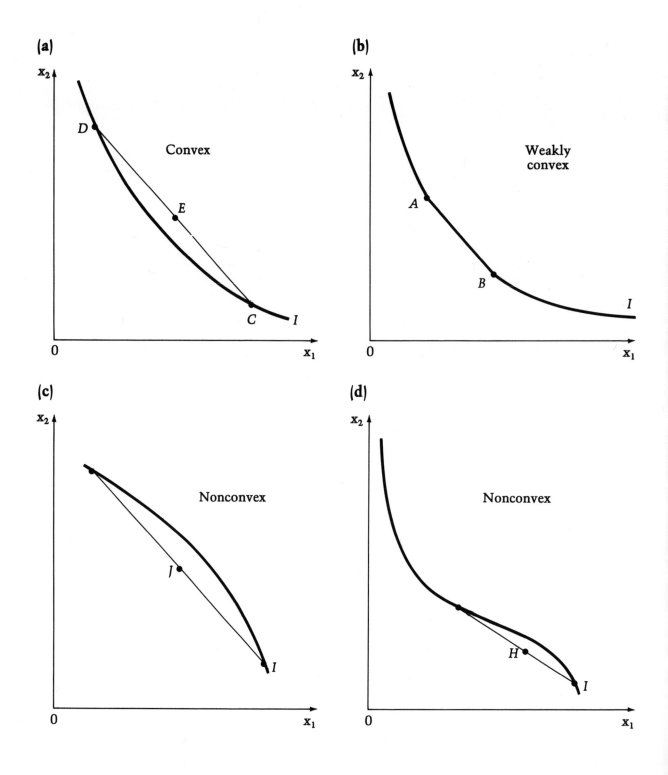

Figure 3.8

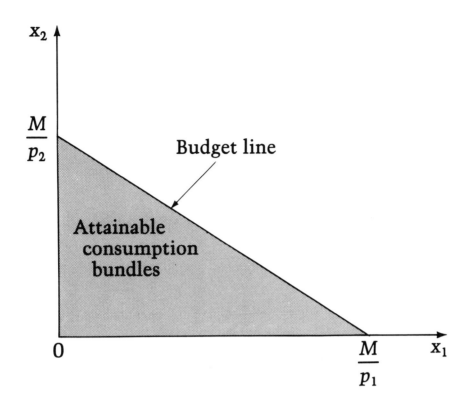

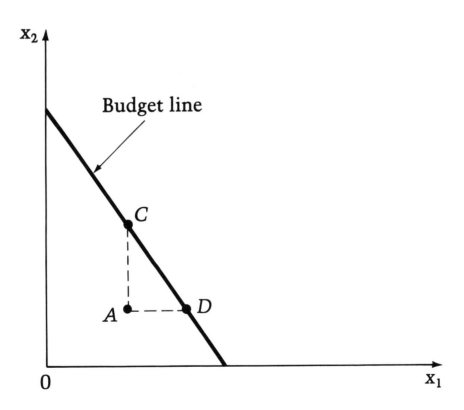

Figures 4.1, 4.2

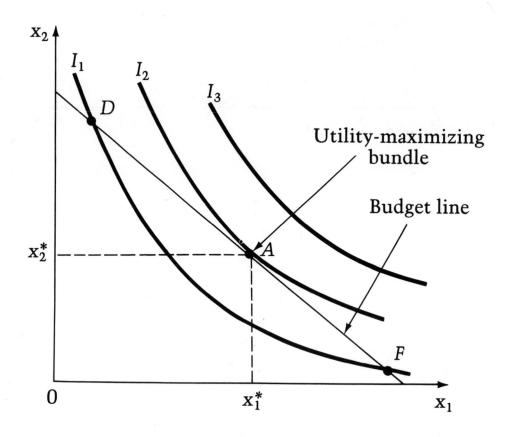

Figure 4.3

(a)

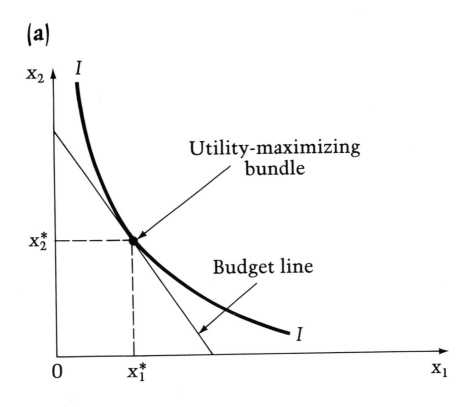

(b)

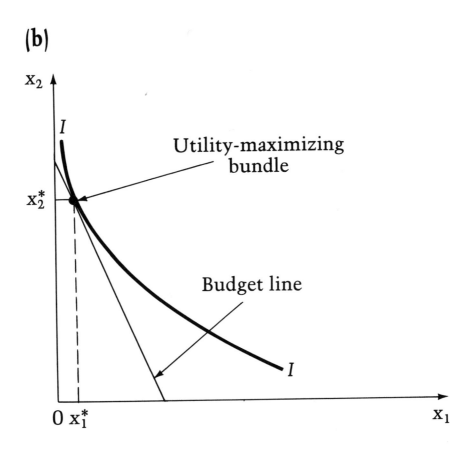

Figure 4.4

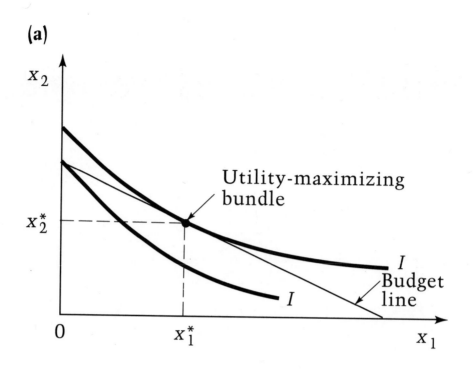

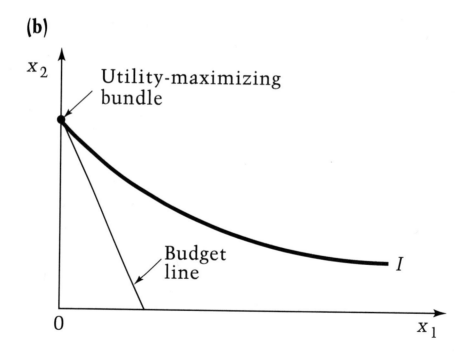

Figure 4.5

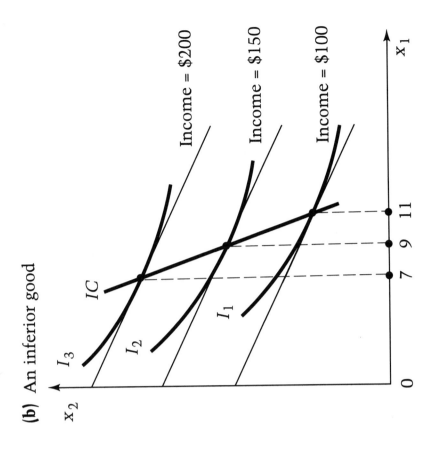
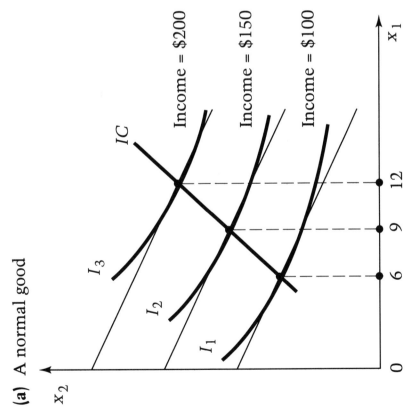

Figure 4.6

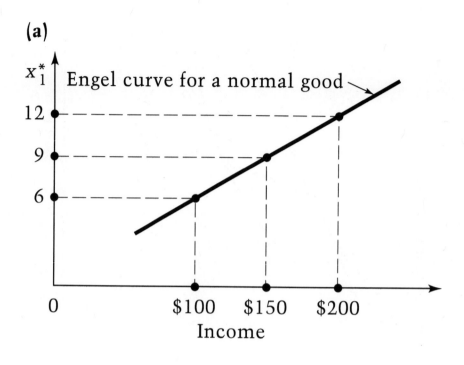

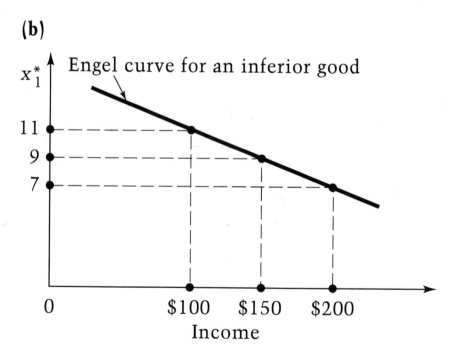

Figure 4.7

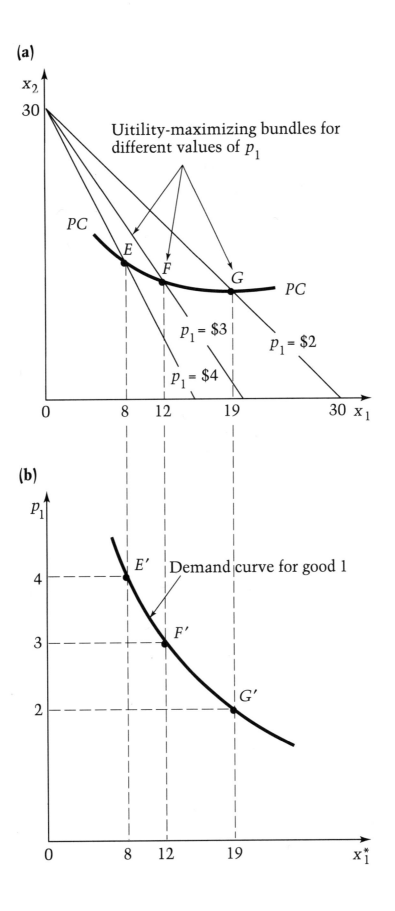

Figure 4.8

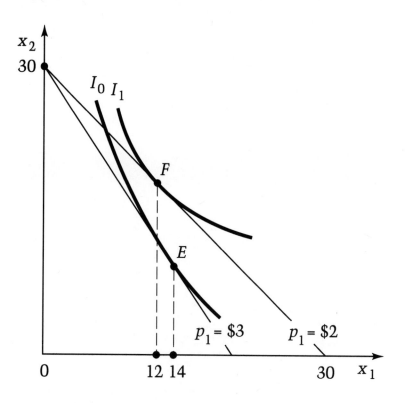

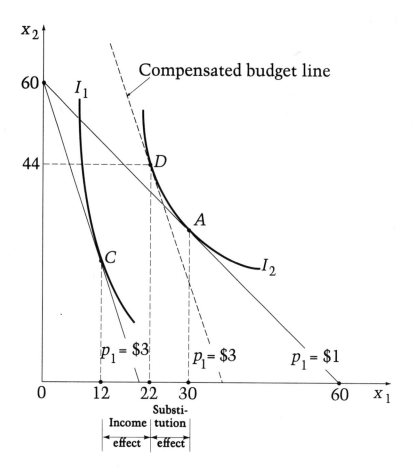

Figures 4.9, 4.10

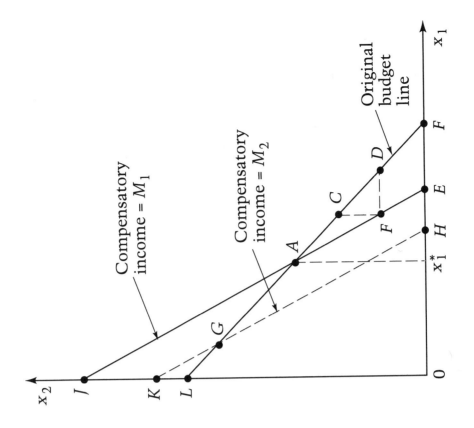

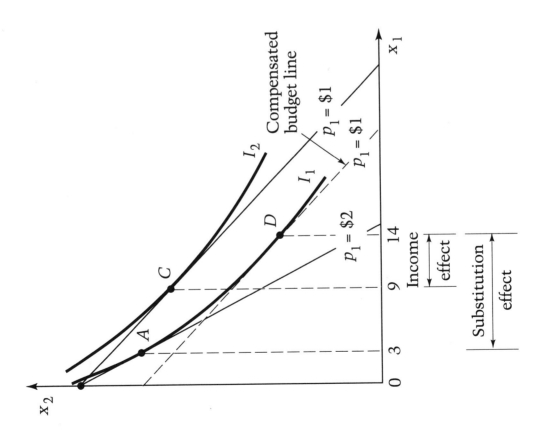

Figures 4.11, 4.12

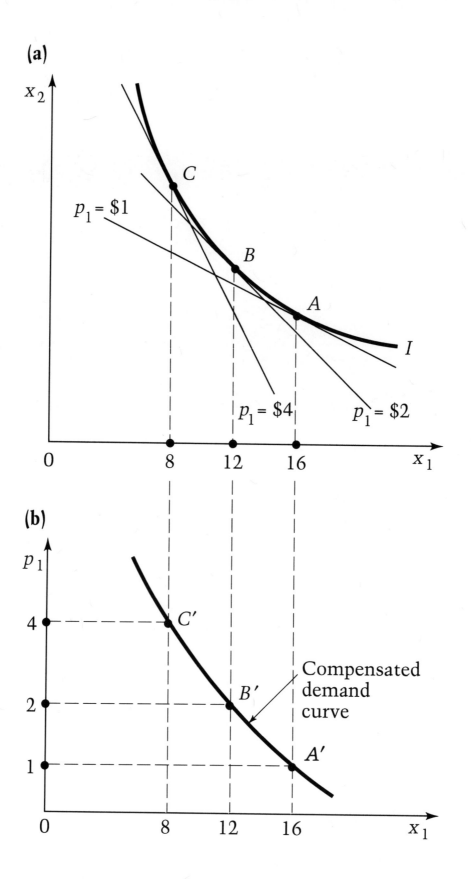

Figure 4.13

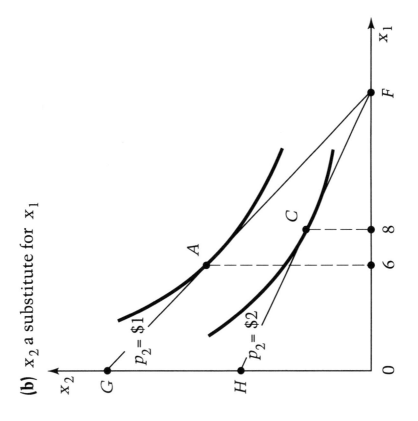
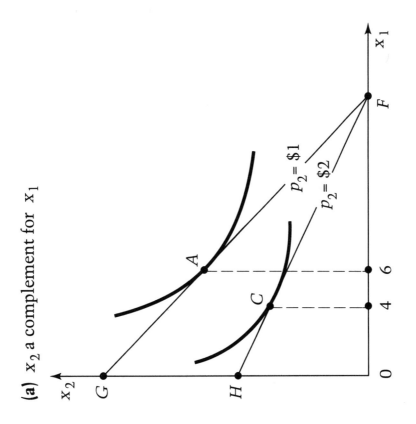

Figure 4.14

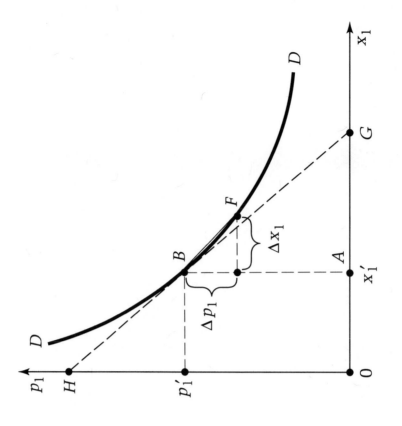

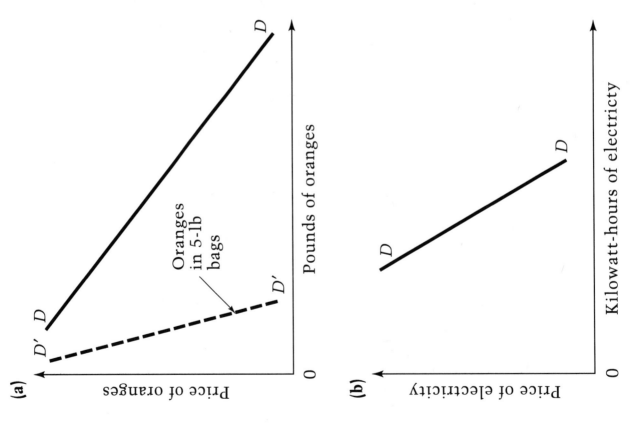

Figures 4.15, 4.16

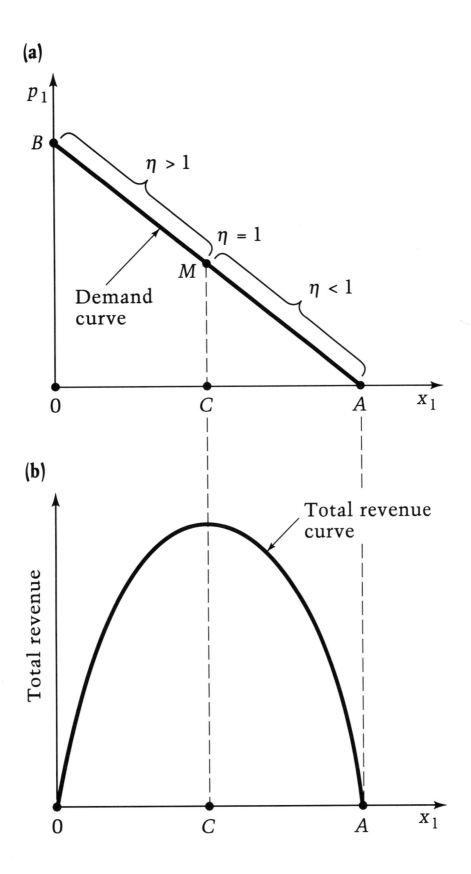

Figure 4.17

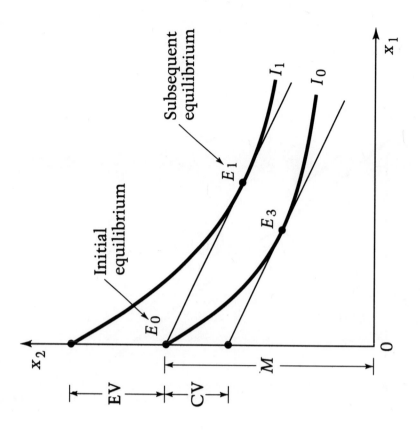
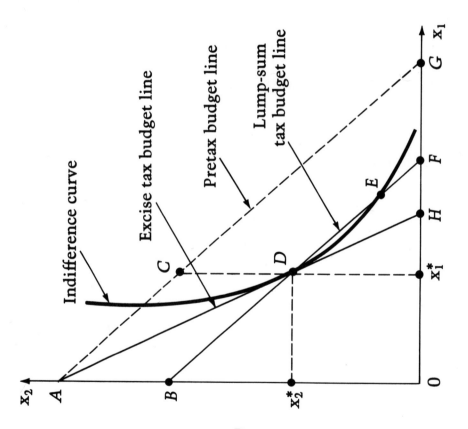

Figures 5.1, 5.2

Eaton and Eaton: MICROECONOMICS, Second Edition

© 1991, W. H. Freeman and Company

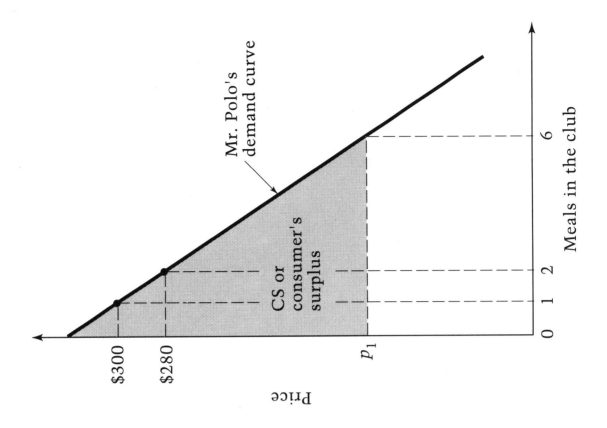

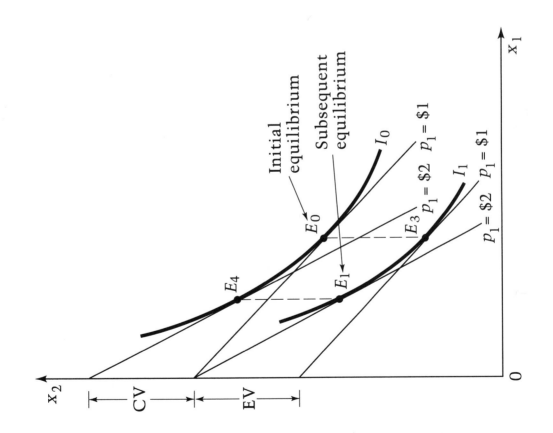

Figures 5.3, 5.4

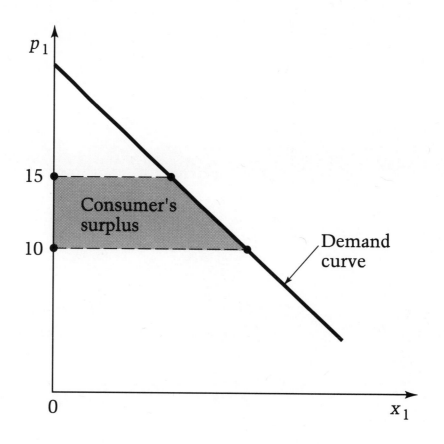

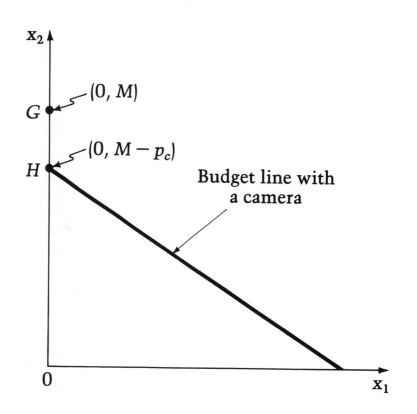

Figures 5.5, 5.6

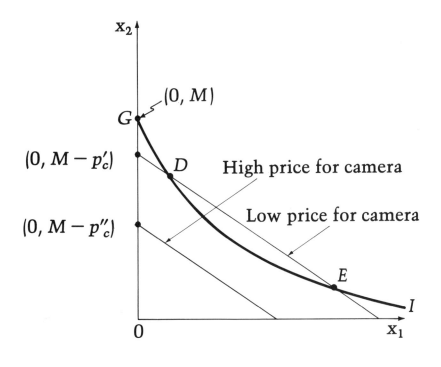

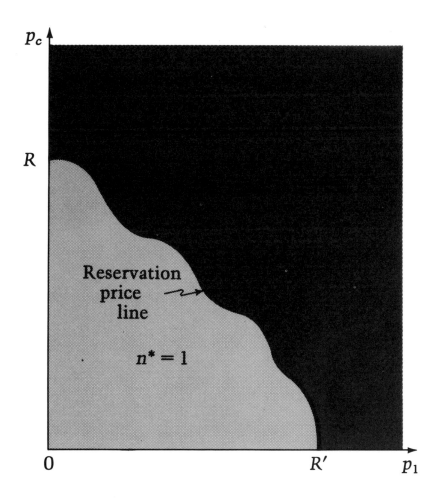

Figures 5.7, 5.8

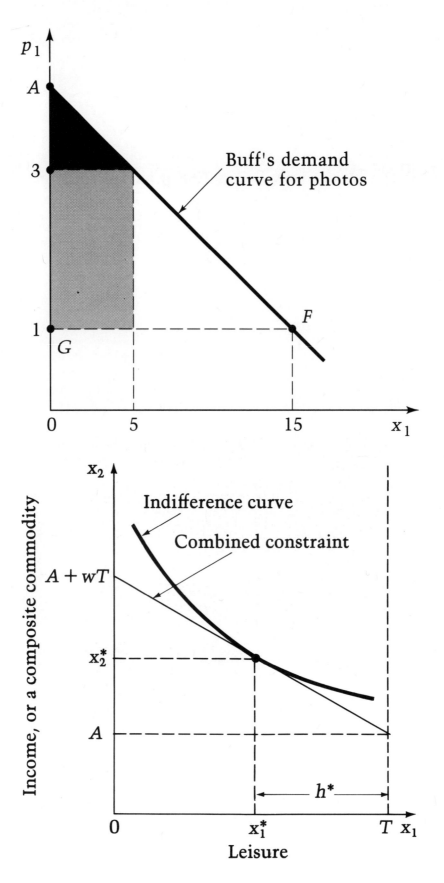

Figures 5.9, 5.10

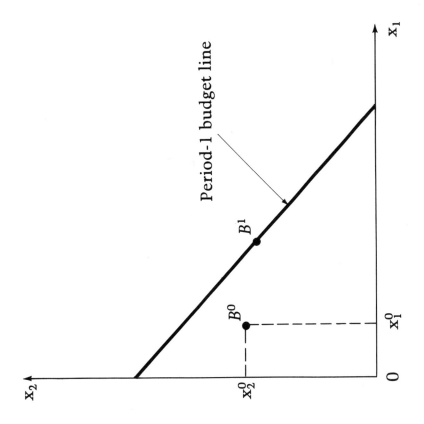

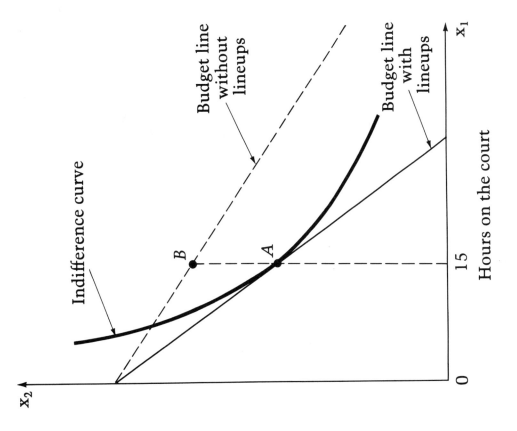

Figures 5.11, 5.12

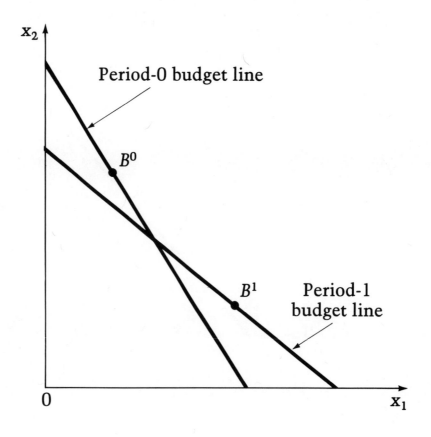
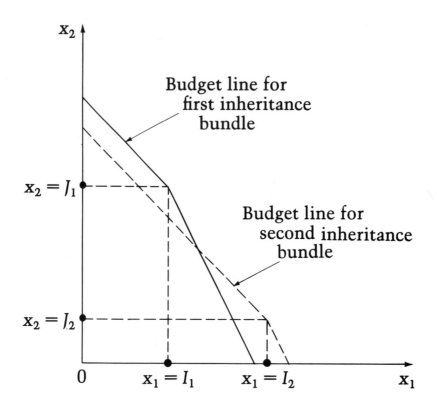

Figures 5.13, 5.14

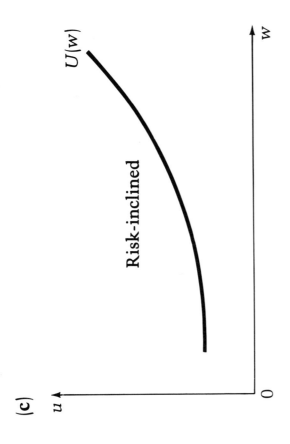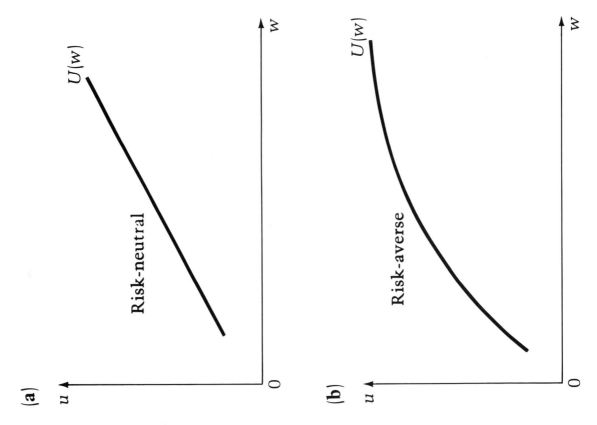

Figure 6.1

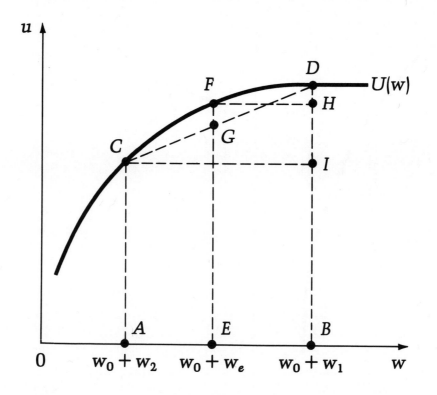

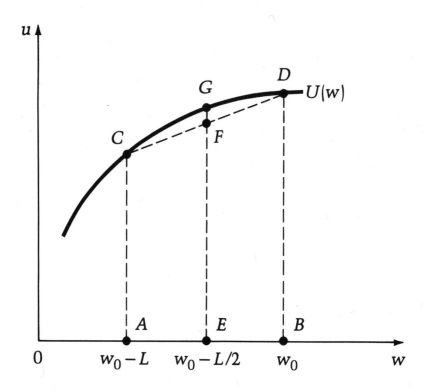

Figures 6.2, 6.3

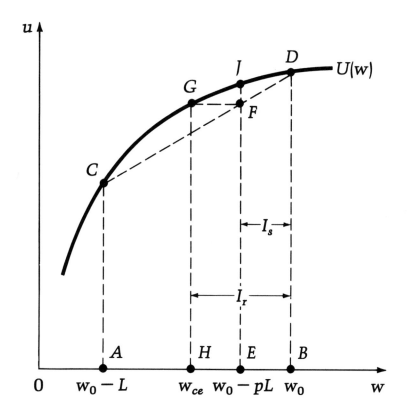

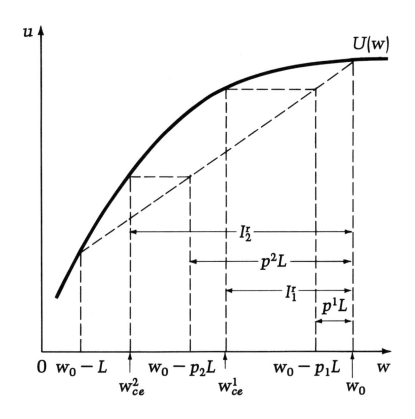

Figures 6.4, 6.5

Eaton and Eaton: MICROECONOMICS, Second Edition

© 1991, W. H. Freeman and Company

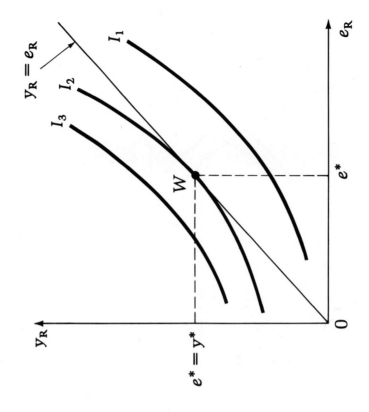
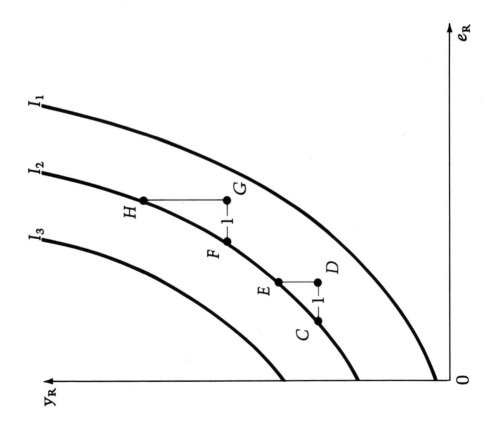

Figures 7.1, 7.2

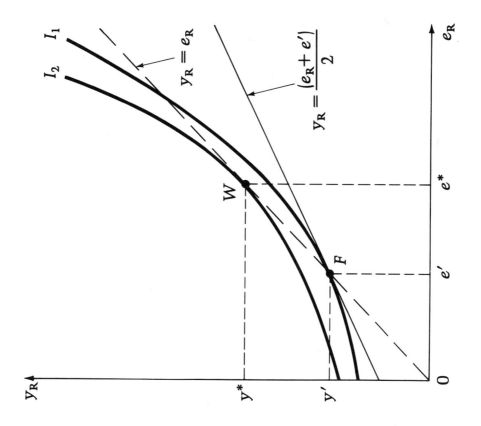

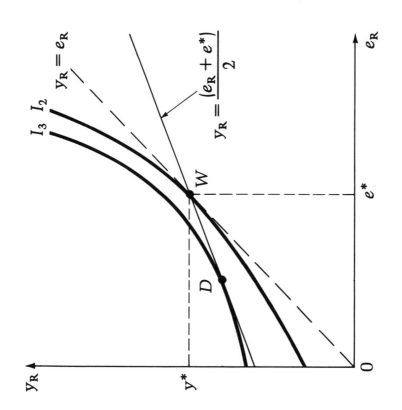

Figures 7.3, 7.4

Eaton and Eaton: MICROECONOMICS, Second Edition

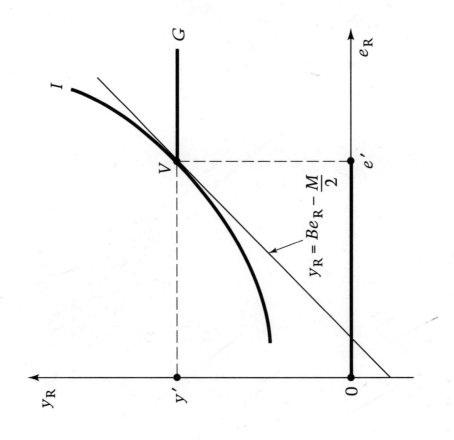

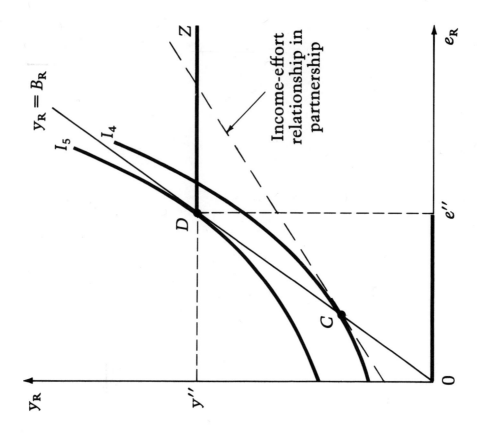

Figures 7.5, 7.6

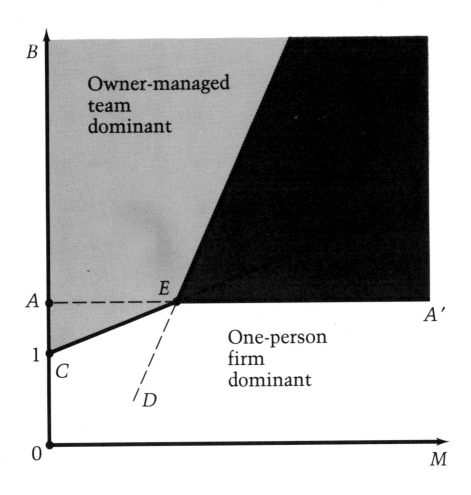

Figure 7.7

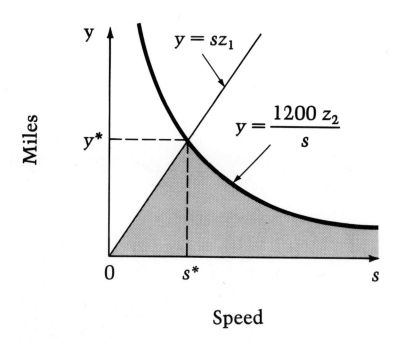

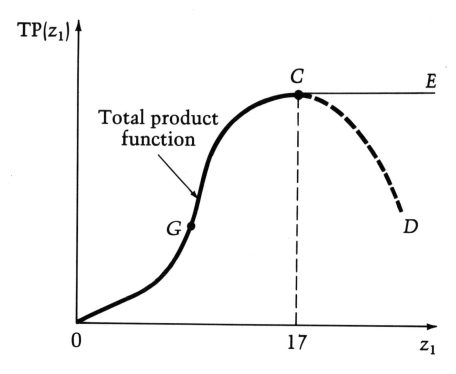

Figures 8.1, 8.2

Eaton and Eaton: MICROECONOMICS, Second Edition

© 1991, W. H. Freeman and Company

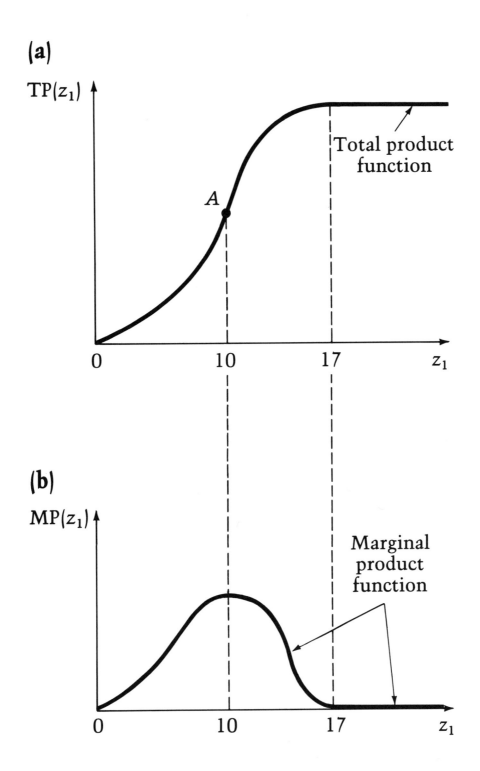

Figure 8.3

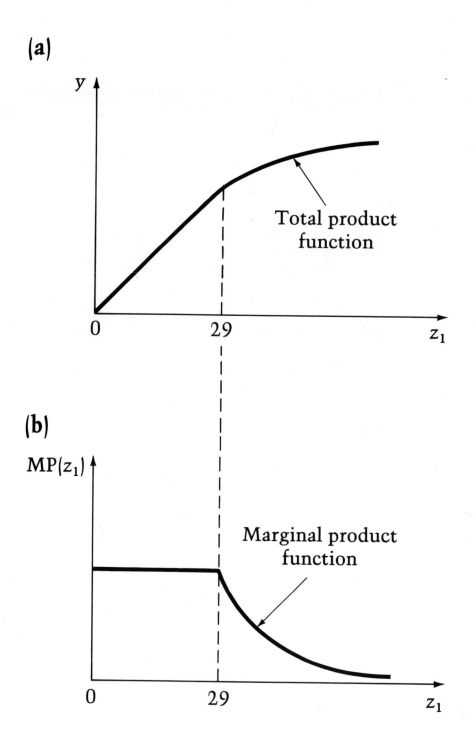

Figure 8.4

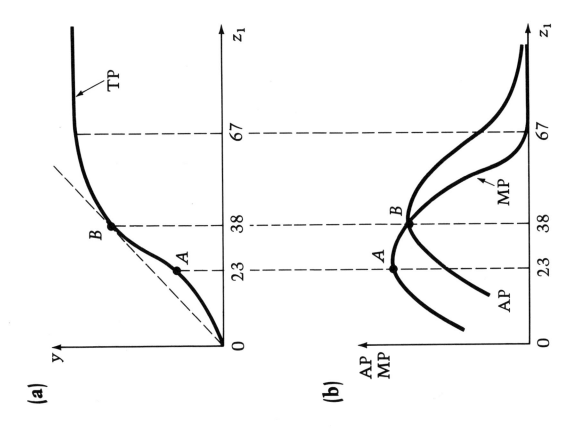

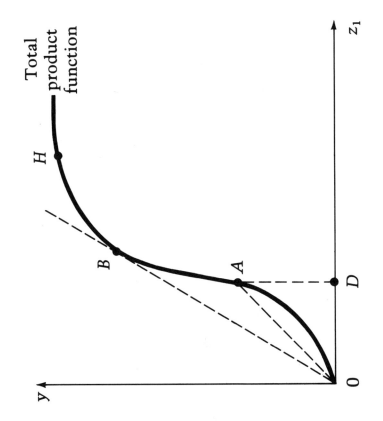

Figures 8.5, 8.6

Eaton and Eaton: MICROECONOMICS, Second Edition

© 1991, W. H. Freeman and Company

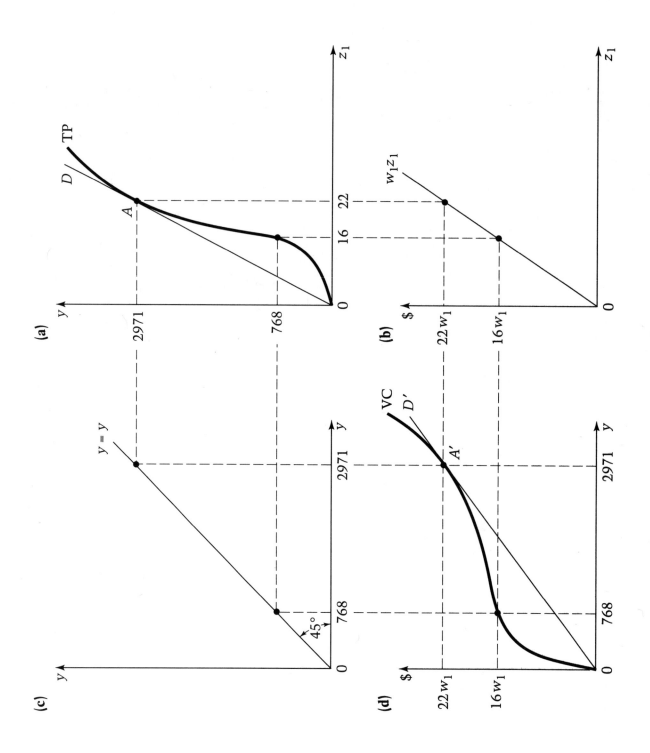

Figure 8.7

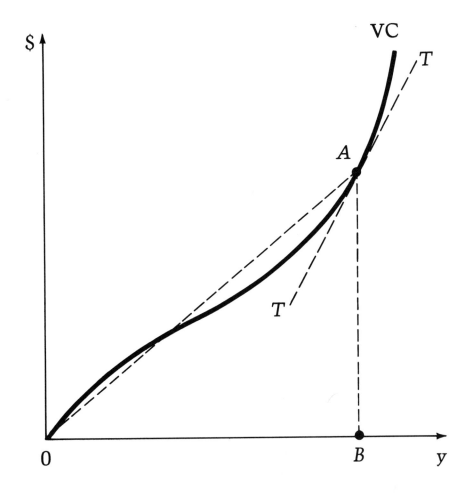

Figure 8.8

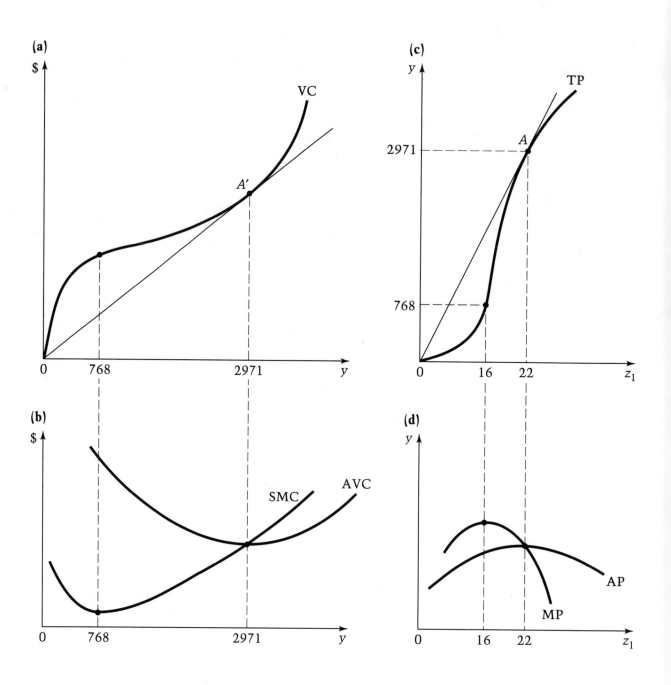

Figure 8.9

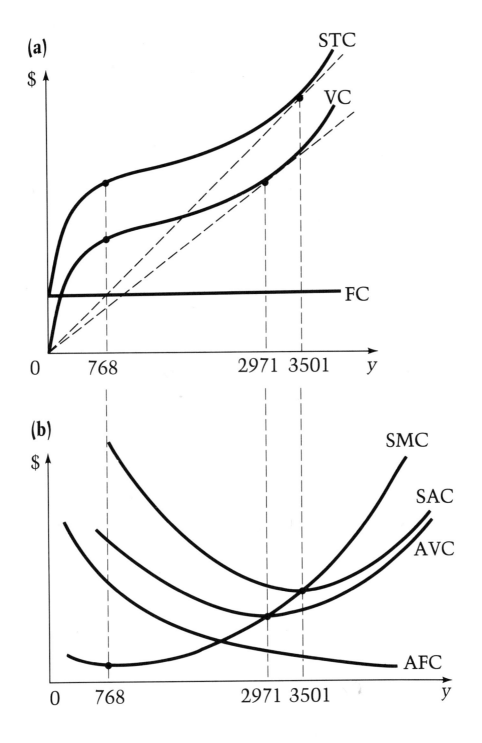

Figure 8.10

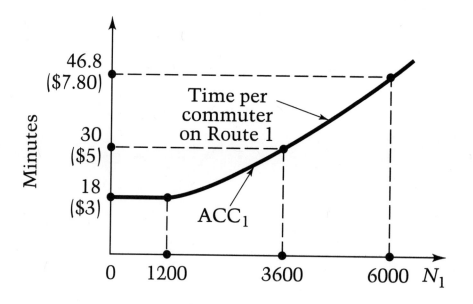
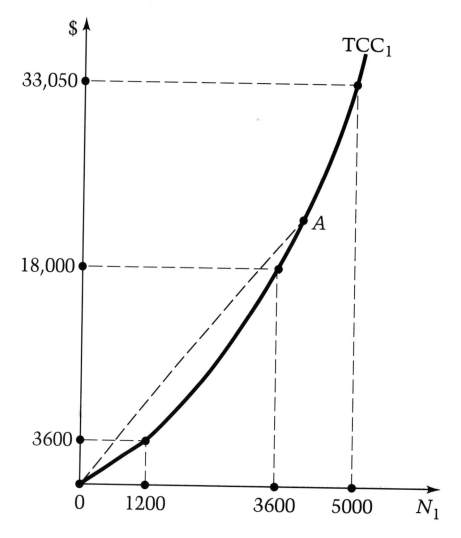

Figures 8.11, 8.12

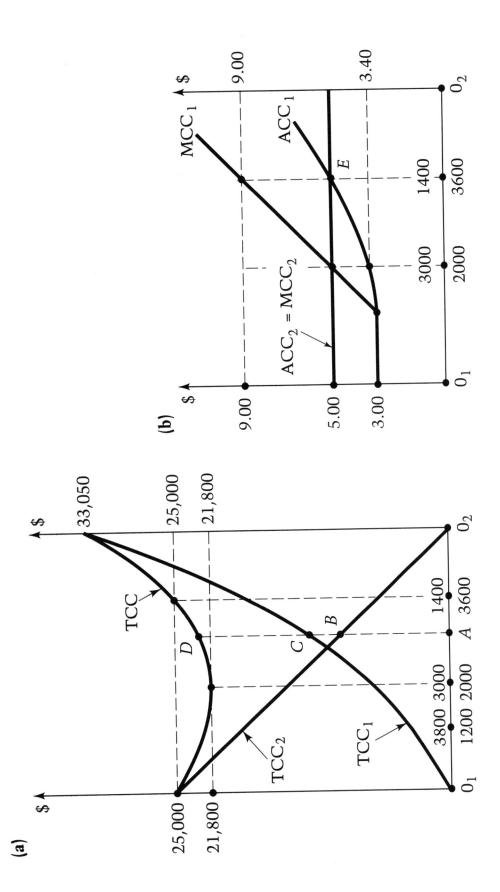

Figure 8.13

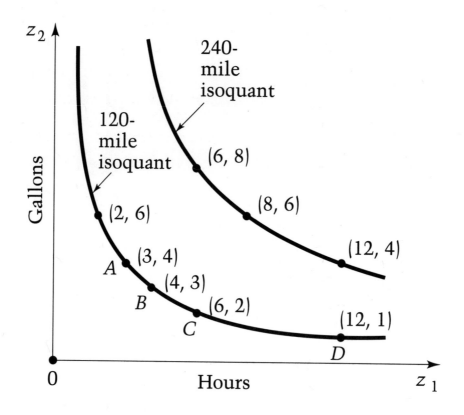

Figure 9.1

Figure 9.2

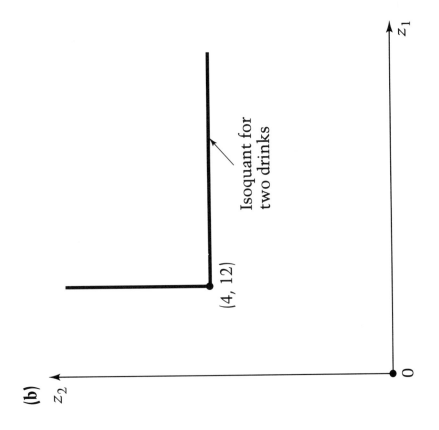

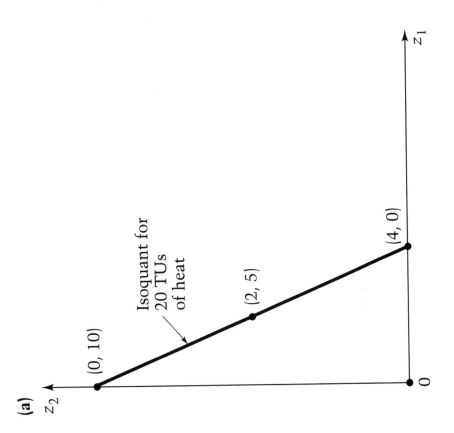

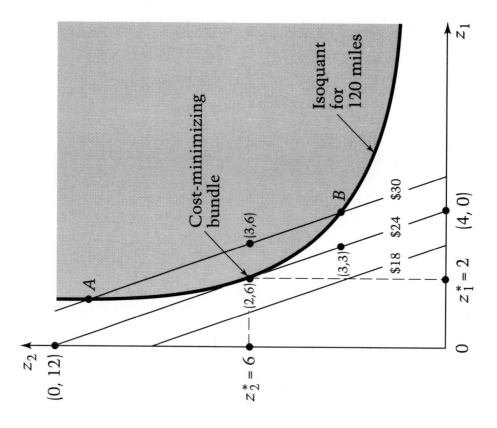

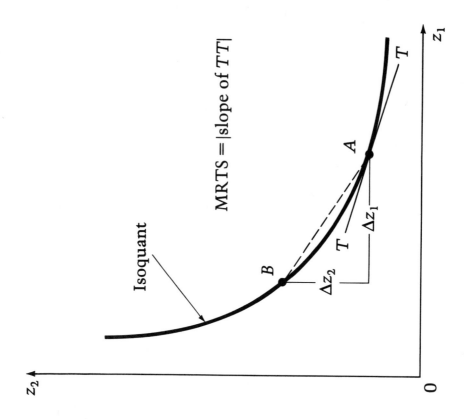

Figures 9.3, 9.4

Eaton and Eaton: MICROECONOMICS, Second Edition

© 1991, W. H. Freeman and Company

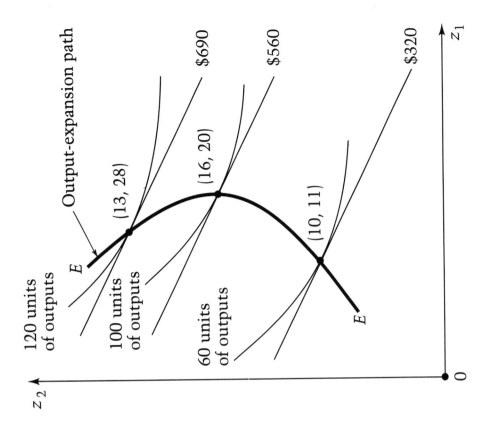

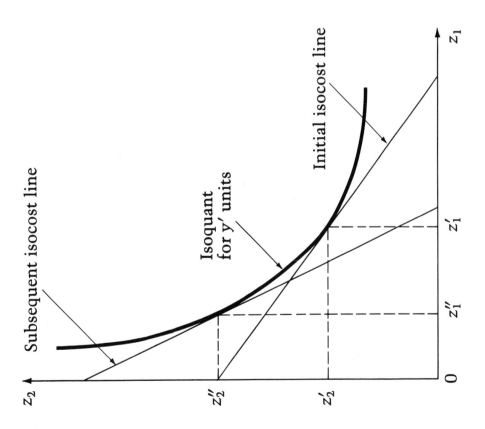

Figures 9.5, 9.6

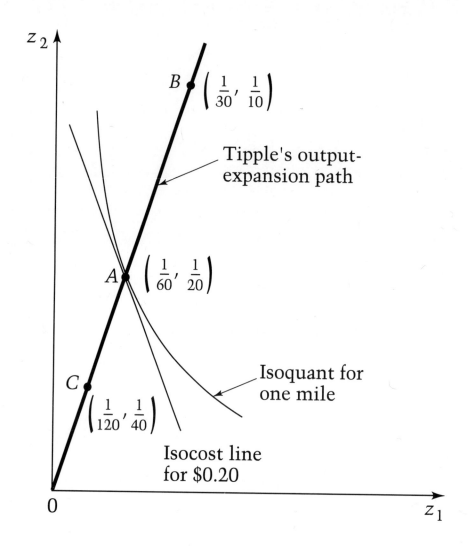

Figure 9.7

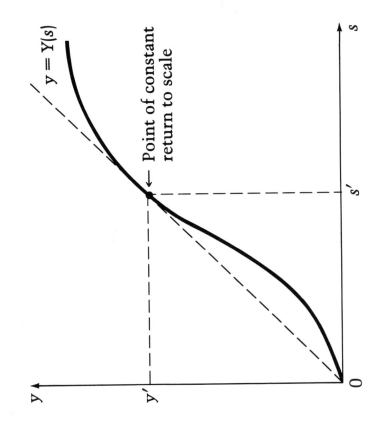

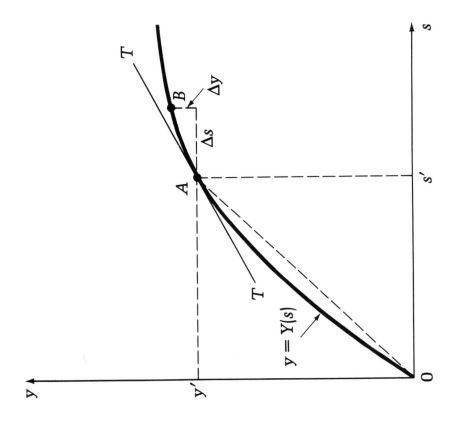

Figures 9.8, 9.9

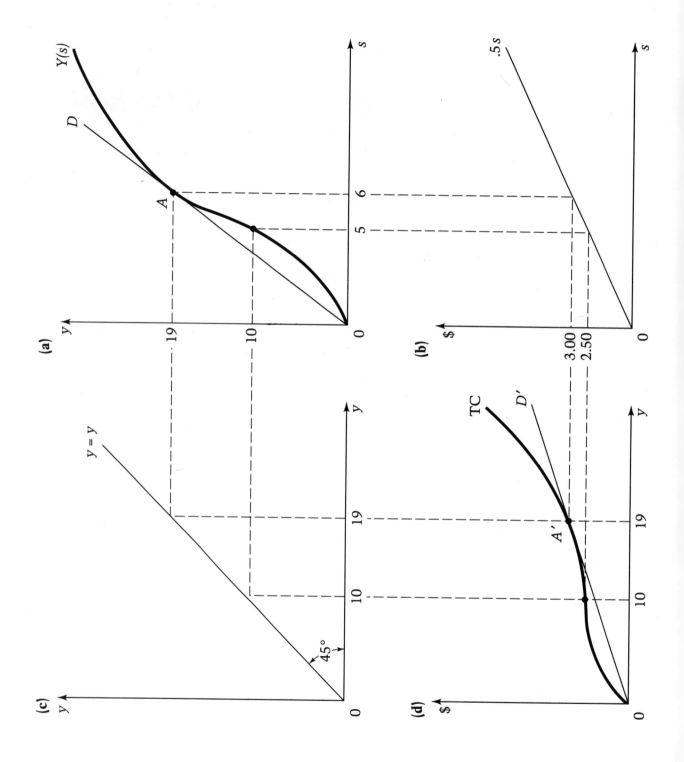

Figure 9.10

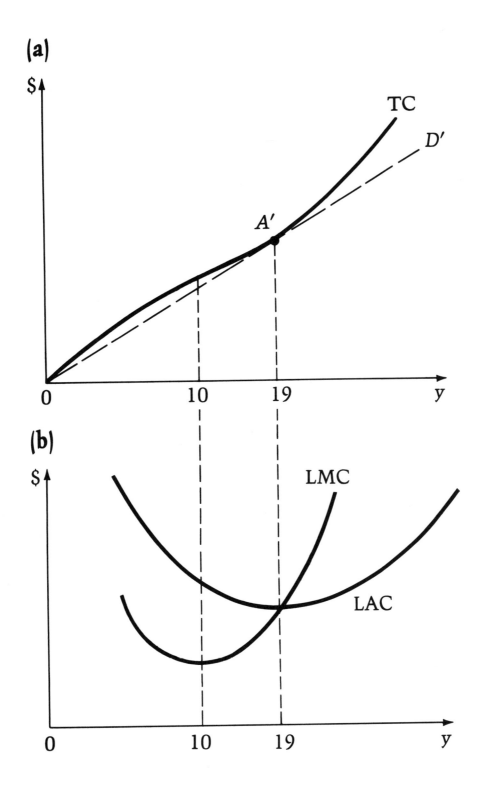

Figure 9.11

(a) Constant returns to scale

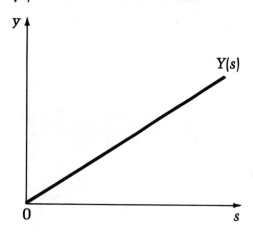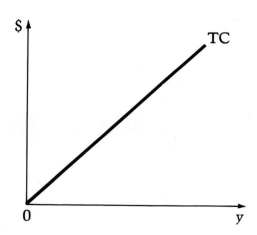

(b) Decreasing returns to scale

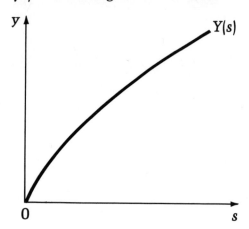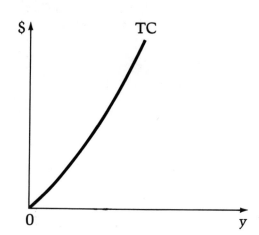

(c) Increasing returns to scale

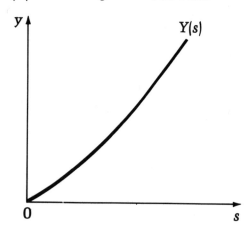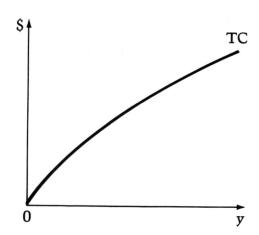

Figure 9.12

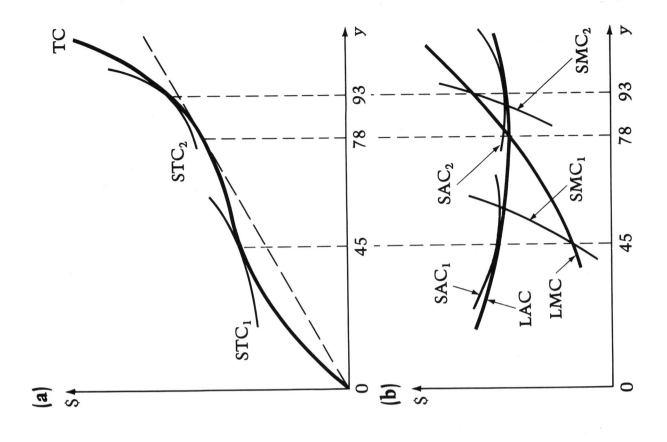
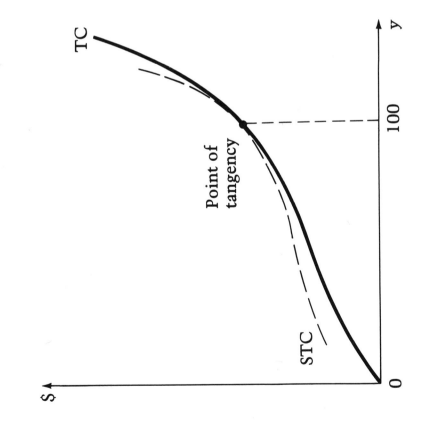

Figures 9.13, 9.14

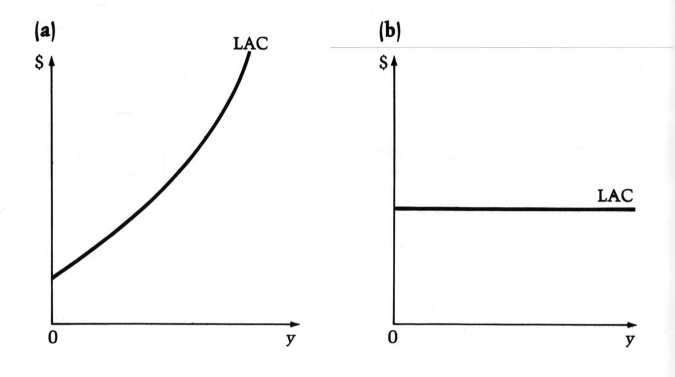
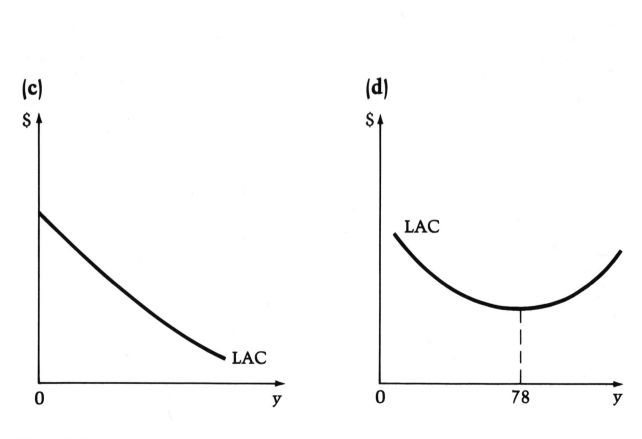

Figure 9.15

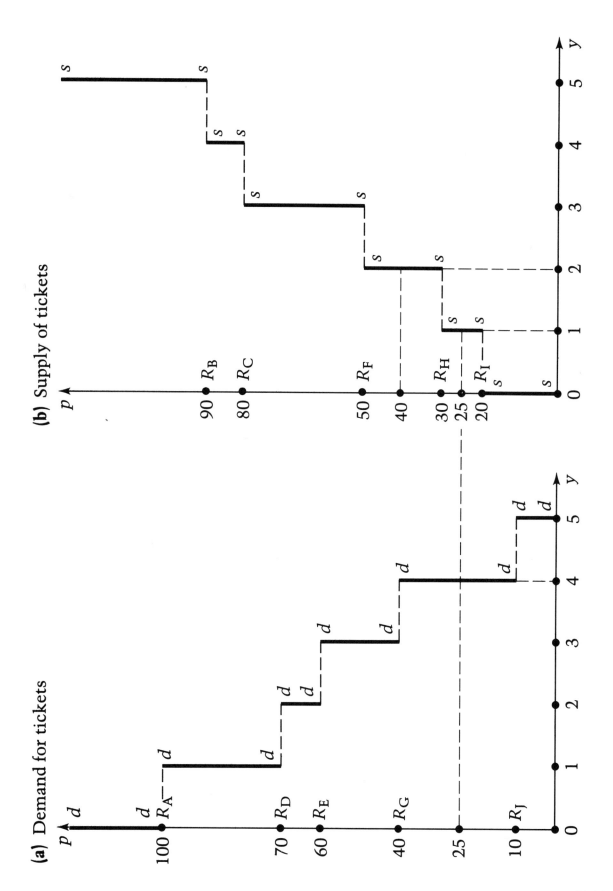

Figure 10.1

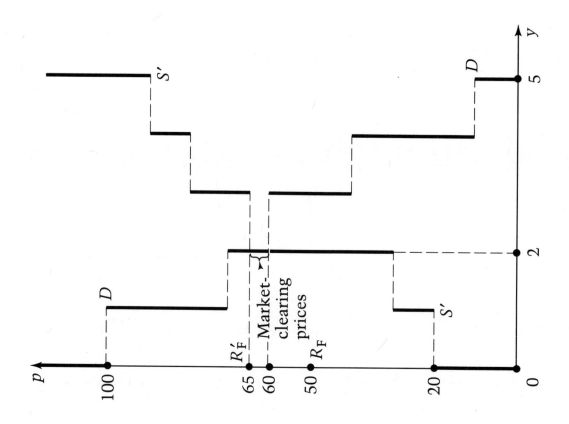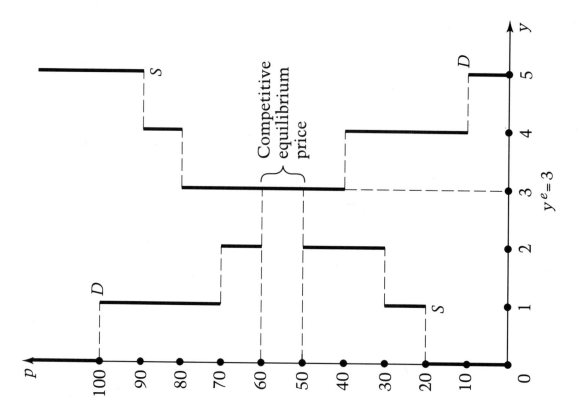

Figures 10.2, 10.3

Eaton and Eaton: MICROECONOMICS, Second Edition
© 1991, W. H. Freeman and Company

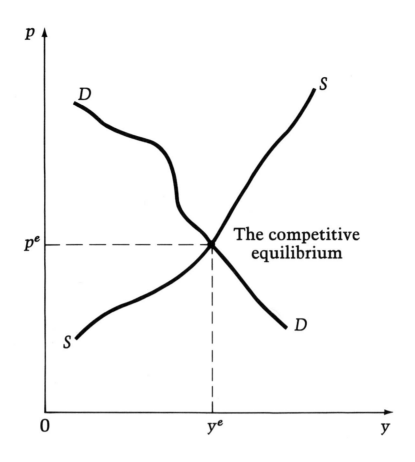

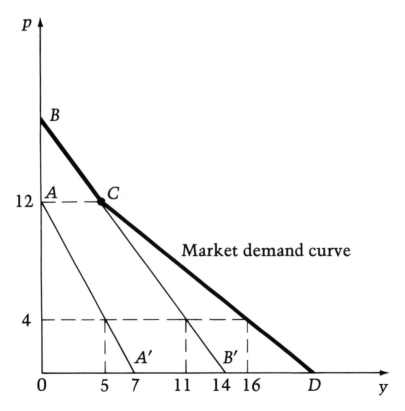

Figures 10.4, 10.5

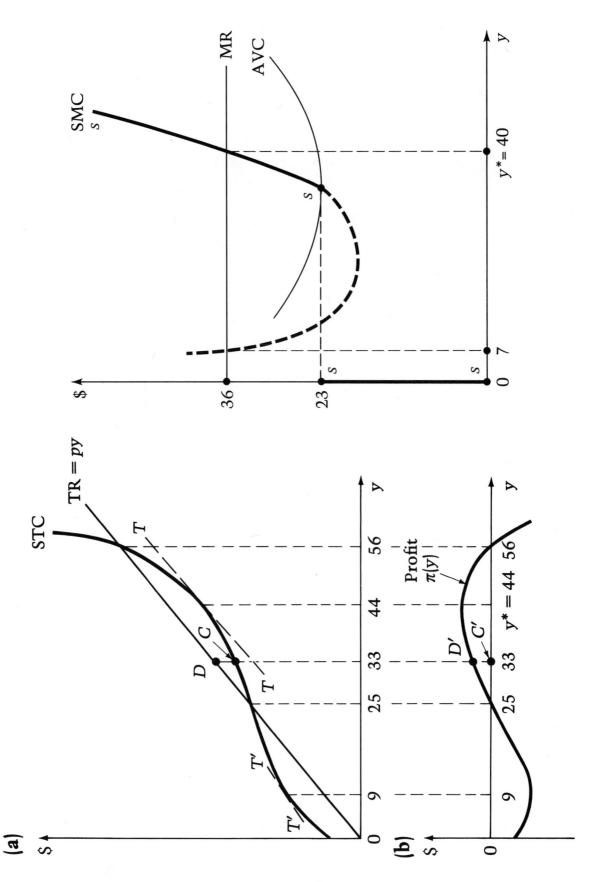

Figures 10.6, 10.7

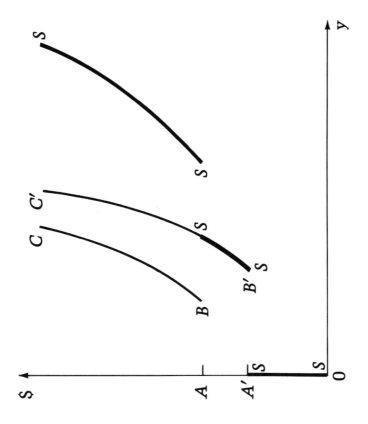
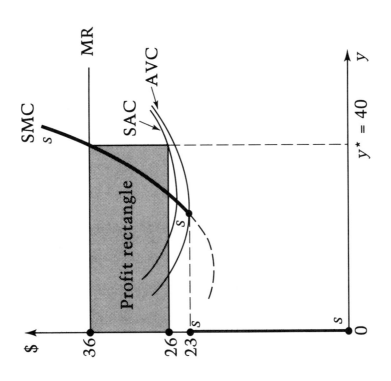

Figures 10.8, 10.9

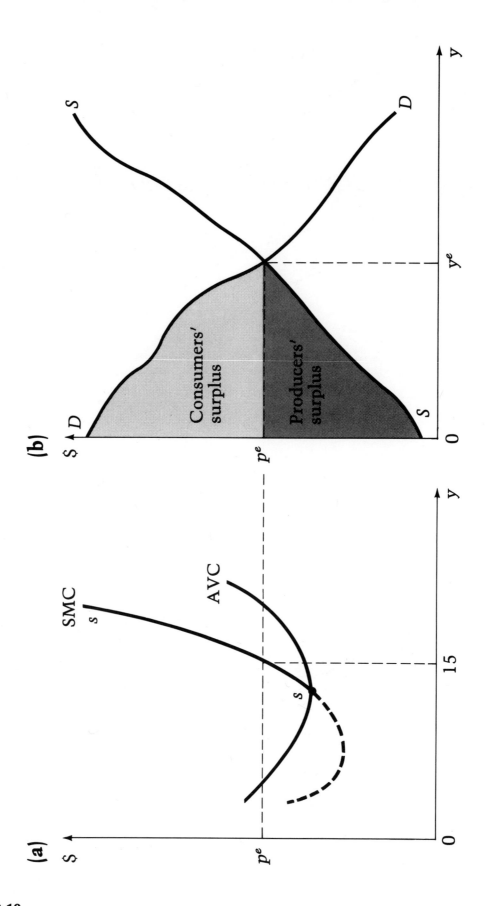

Figure 10.10

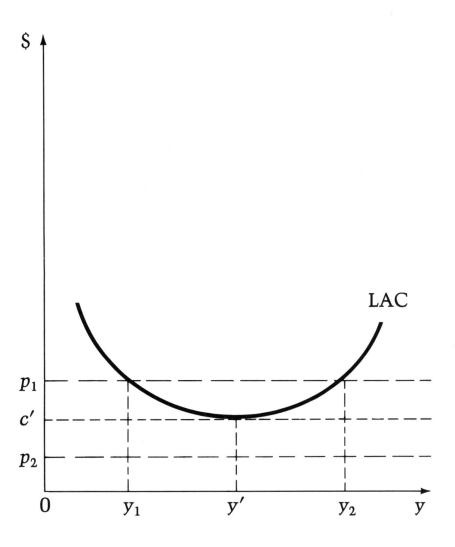

Figure 10.11

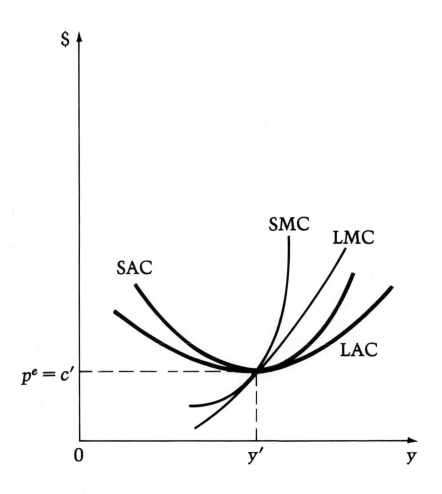
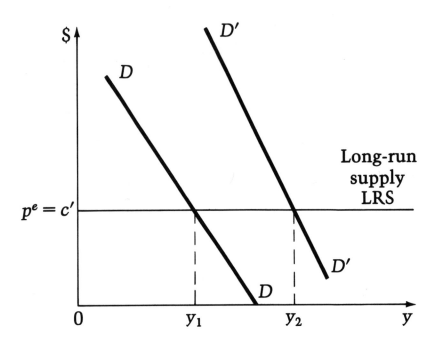

Figures 10.12, 10.13

Eaton and Eaton: MICROECONOMICS, Second Edition

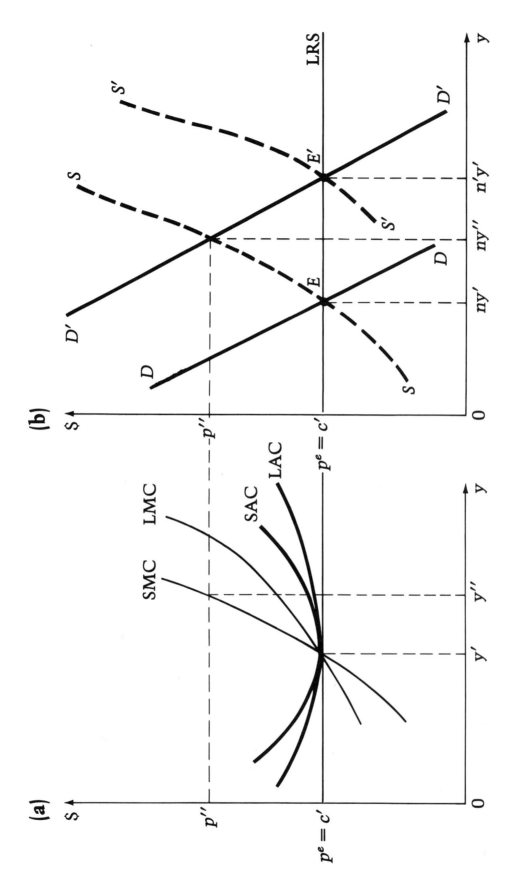

Figure 10.14

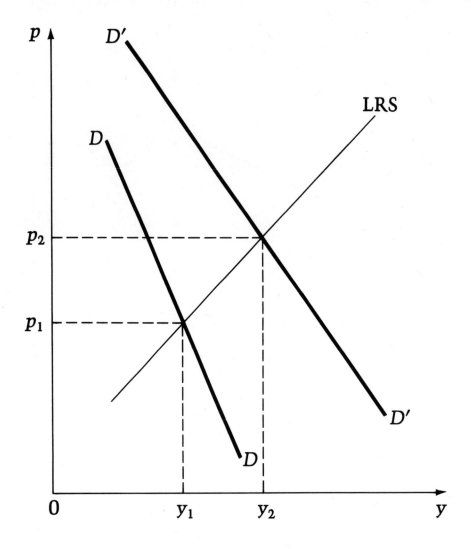

Figure 10.15

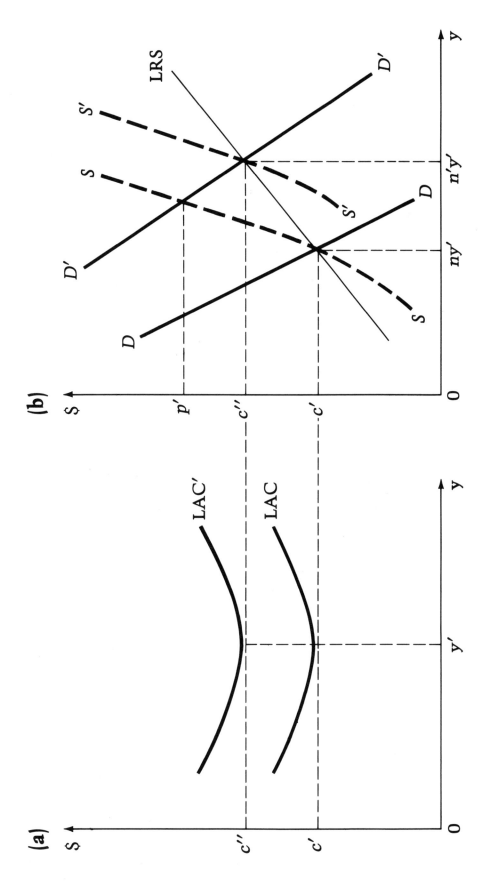

Figure 10.16

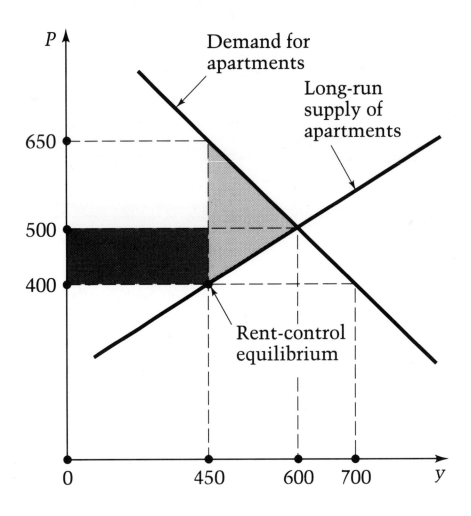

Figure 10.17

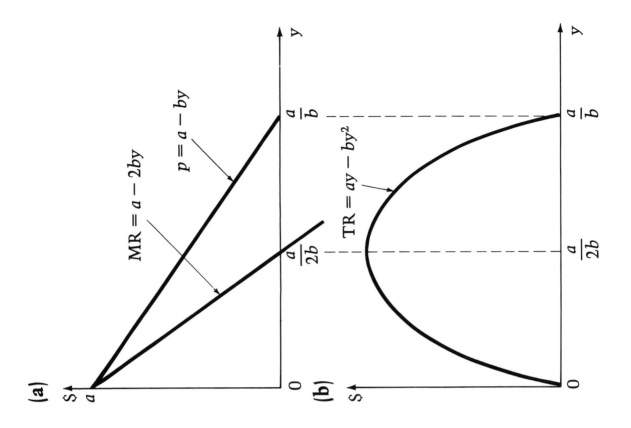

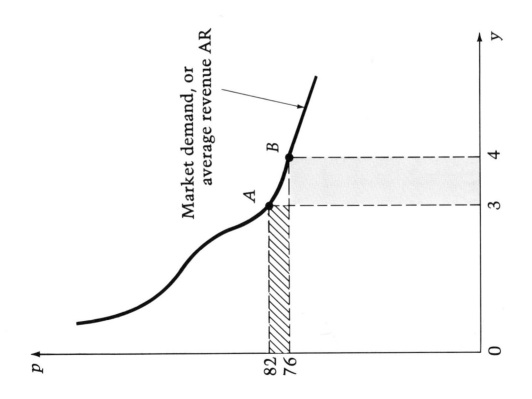

Figures 11.1, 11.2

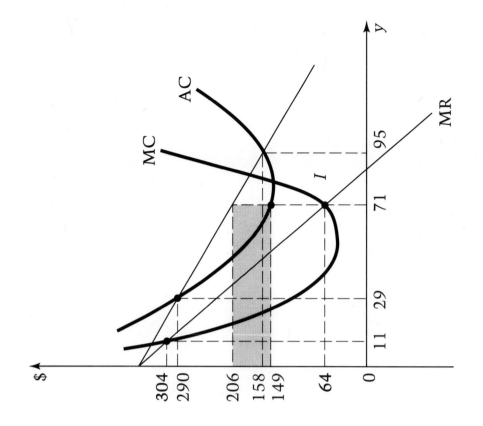
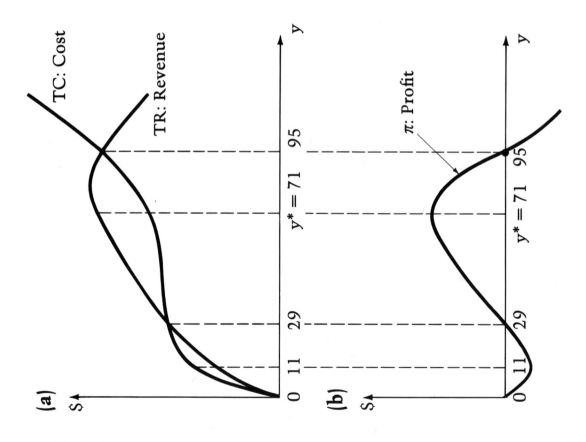

Figures 11.3, 11.4

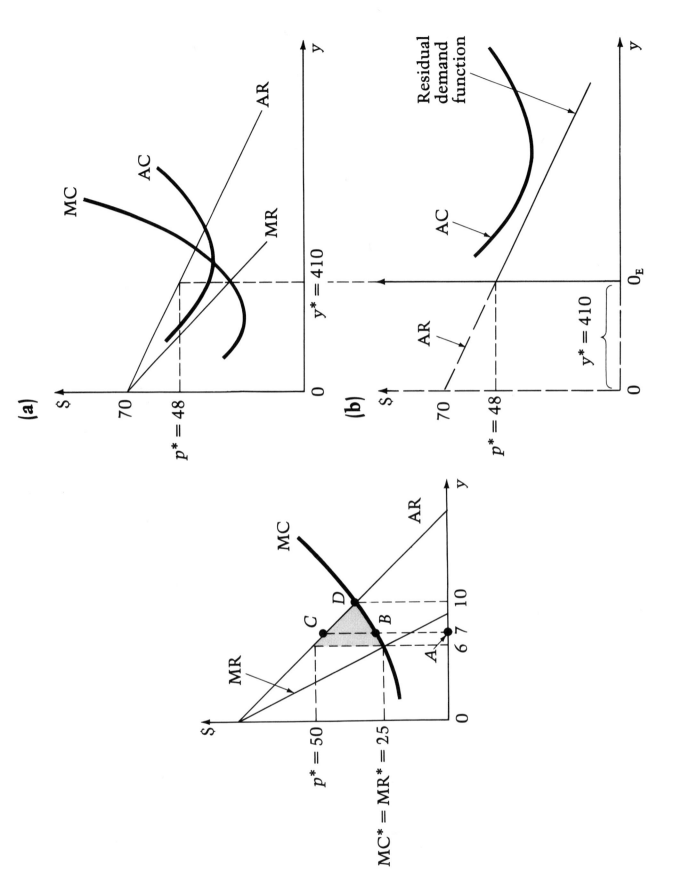

Figures 11.5, 11.6

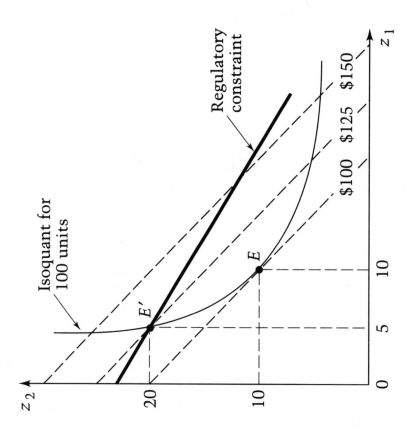

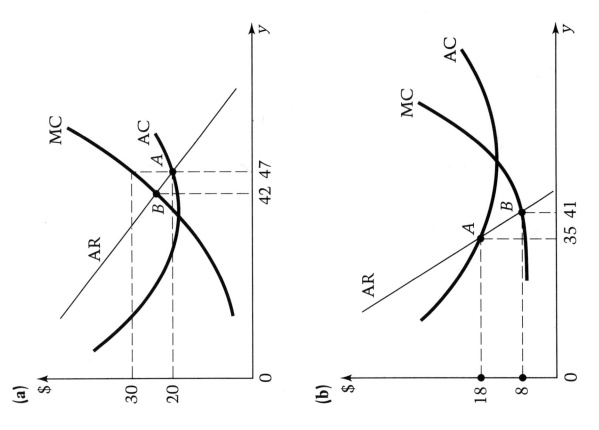

Figures 11.7, 11.8

Eaton and Eaton: MICROECONOMICS, Second Edition

© 1991, W. H. Freeman and Company

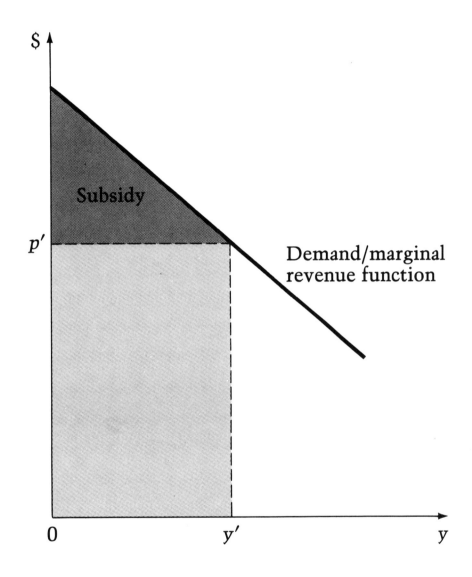

Figure 11.9

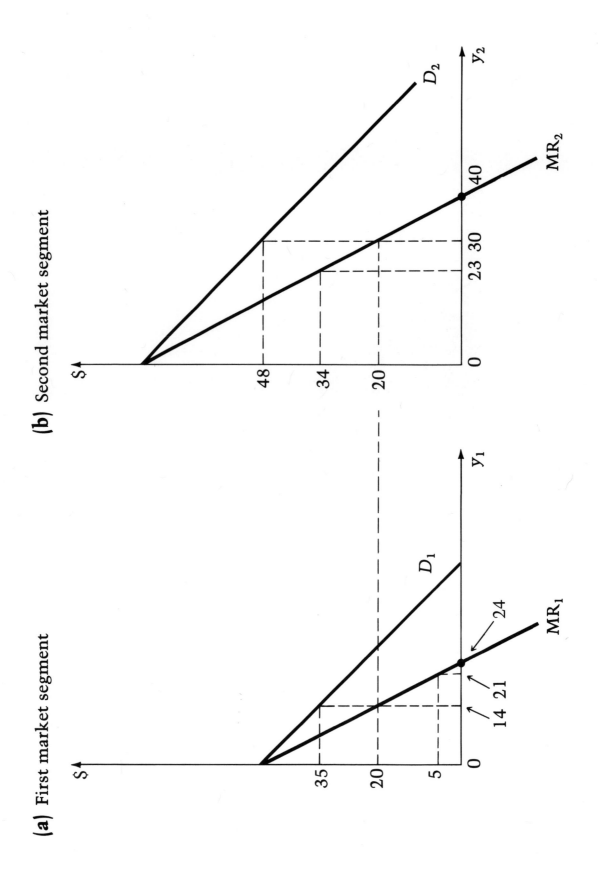

Figure 11.10

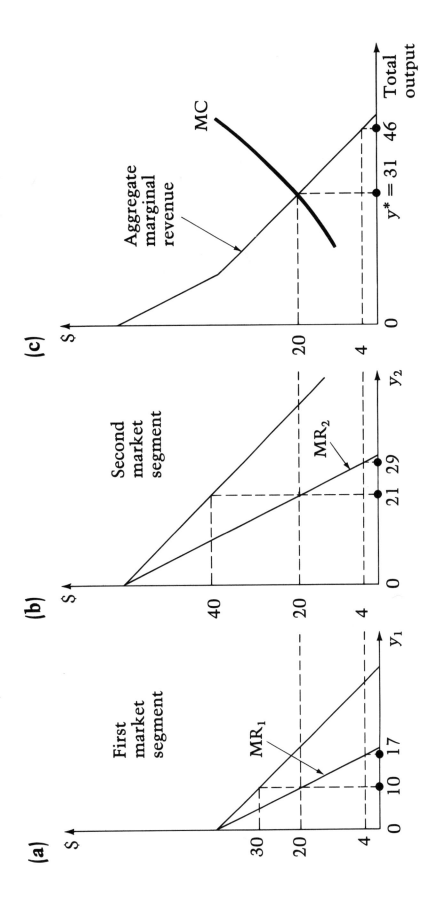

Figure 11.11

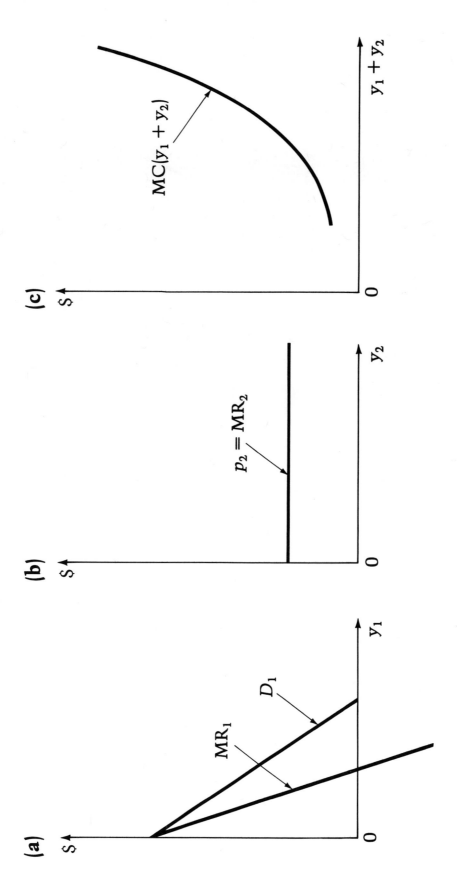

Figure 11.12

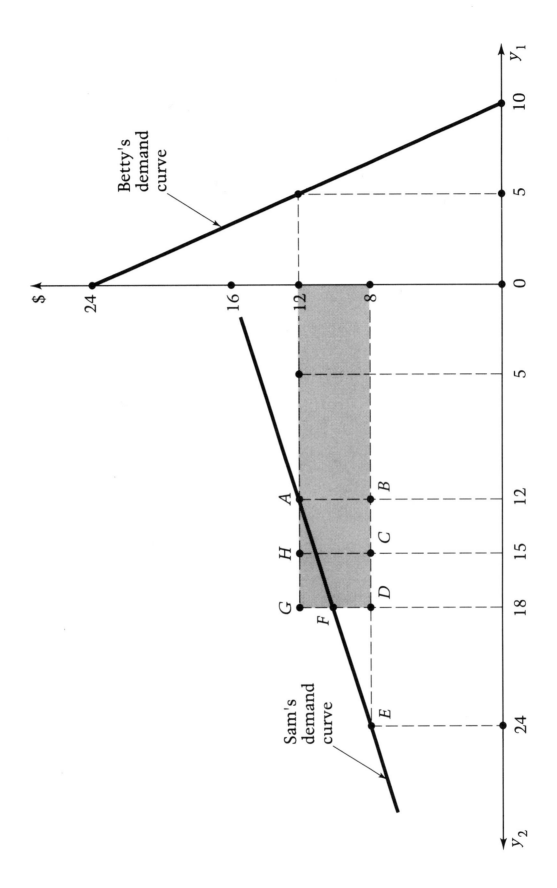

Figure 11.13

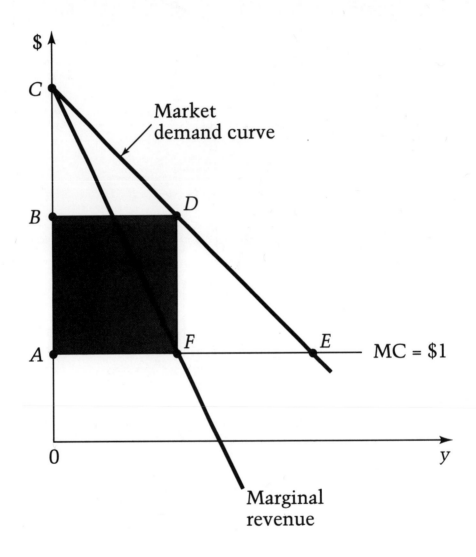

Figure 11.14

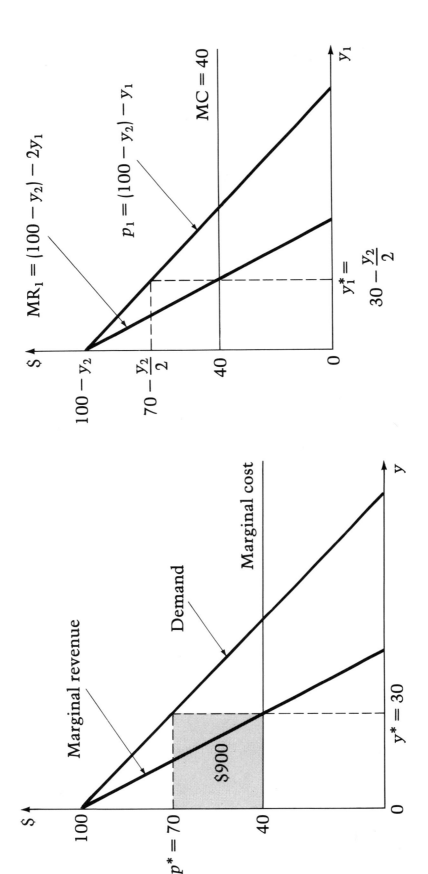

Figures 12.1, 12.2

Eaton and Eaton: MICROECONOMICS, Second Edition

© 1991, W. H. Freeman and Company

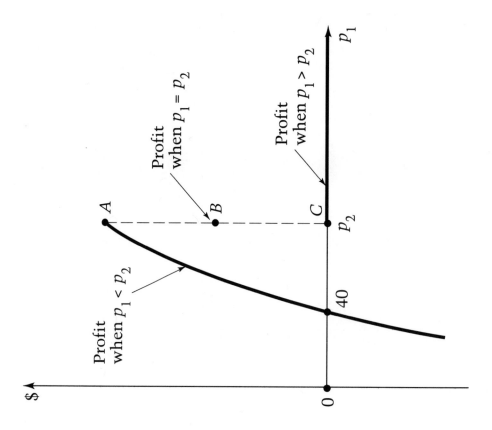

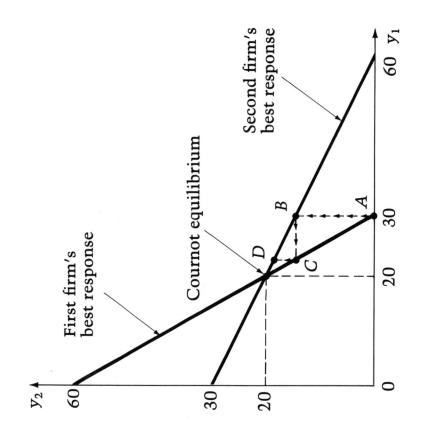

Figures 12.3, 12.4

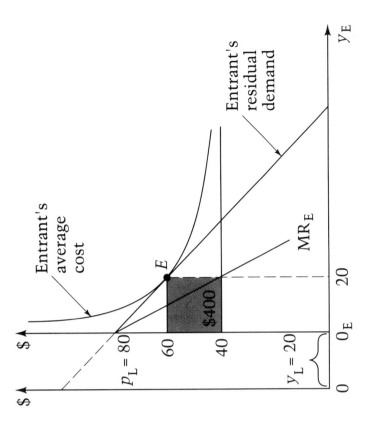
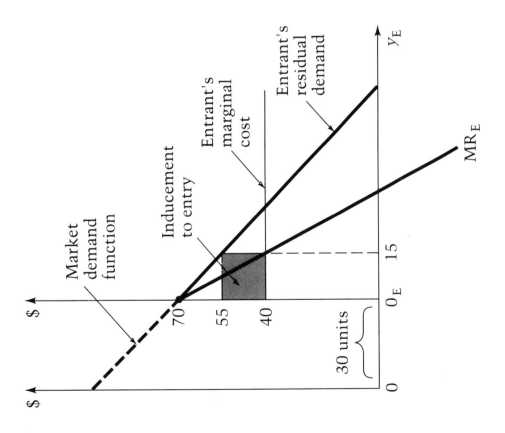

Figures 12.5, 12.6

Eaton and Eaton: MICROECONOMICS, Second Edition

© 1991, W. H. Freeman and Company

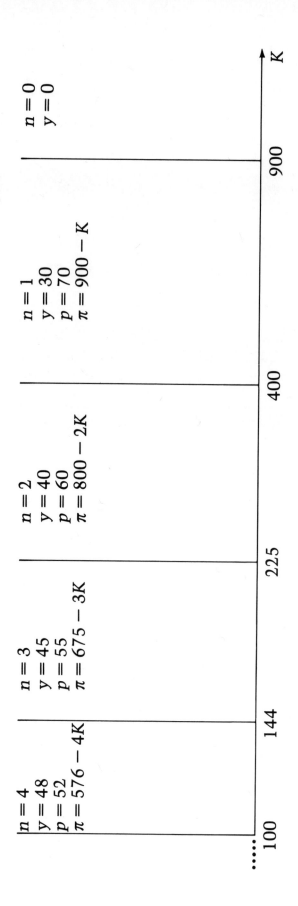

Figure 12.7

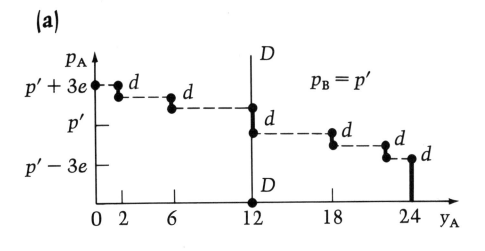

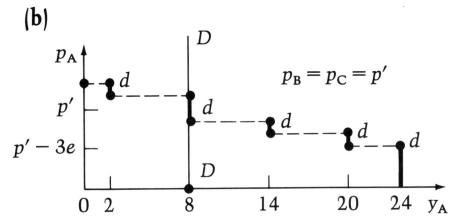

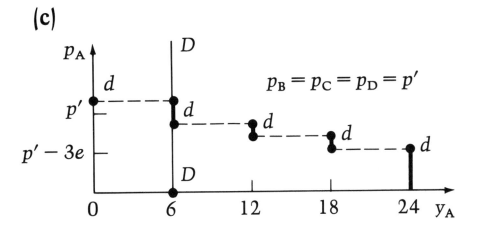

Figure 13.1

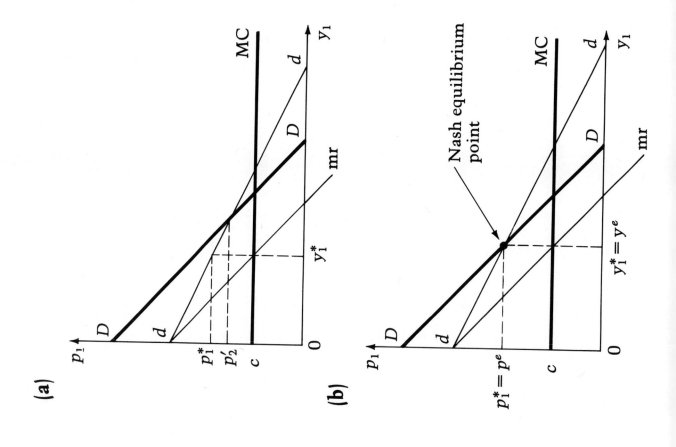
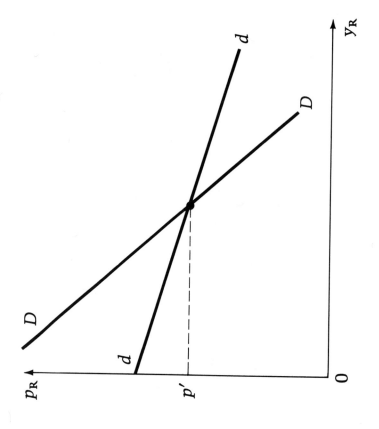

Figures 13.2, 13.3

Eaton and Eaton: MICROECONOMICS, Second Edition
© 1991, W. H. Freeman and Company

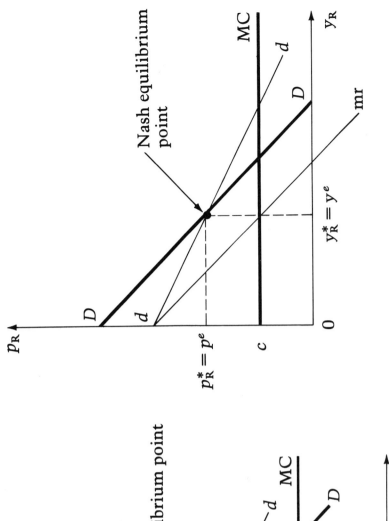
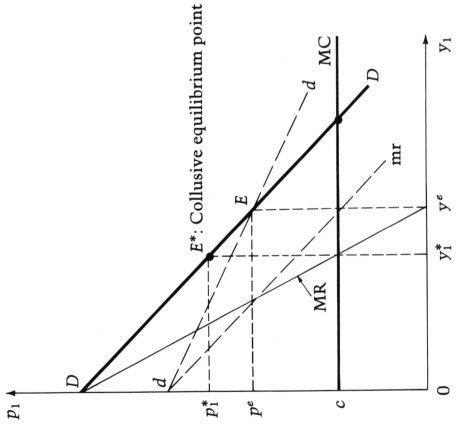

Figures 13.4, 13.5

Eaton and Eaton: MICROECONOMICS, Second Edition

© 1991, W. H. Freeman and Company

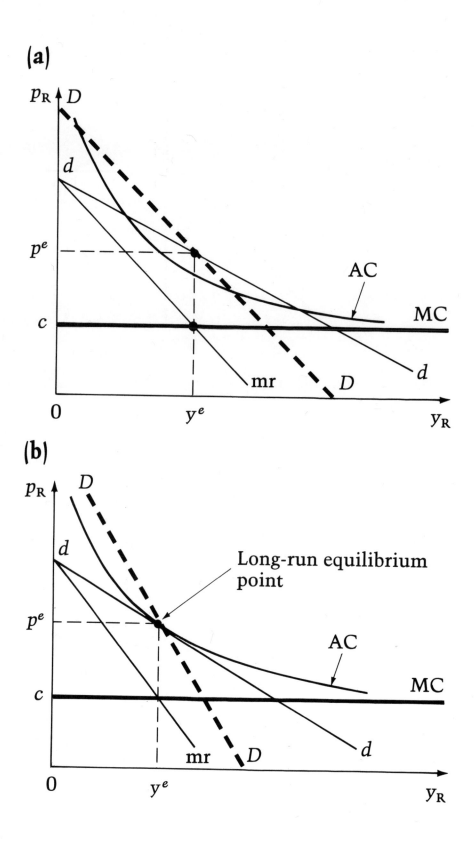

Figure 13.6

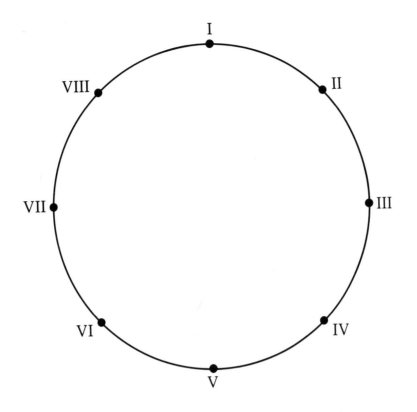

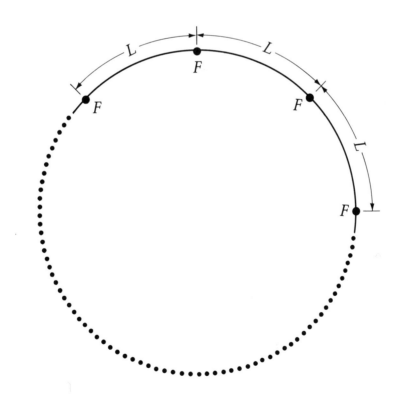

Figures 13.7, 13.8

Eaton and Eaton: MICROECONOMICS, Second Edition

© 1991, W. H. Freeman and Company

Pages 370, 371

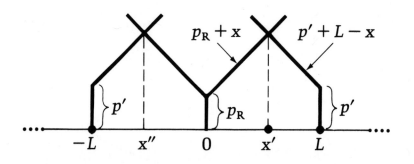

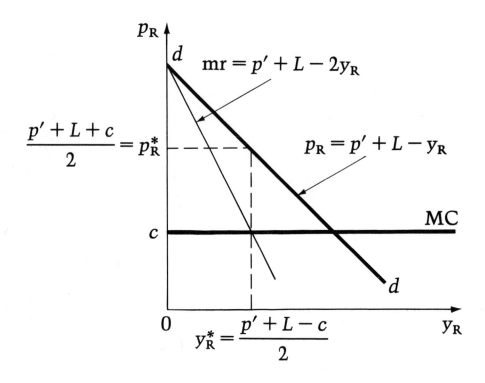

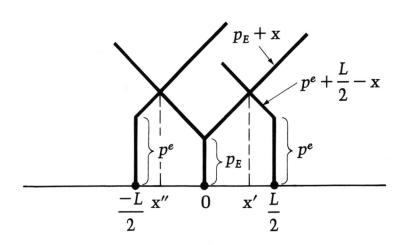

Figures 13.9, 13.10, 13.11

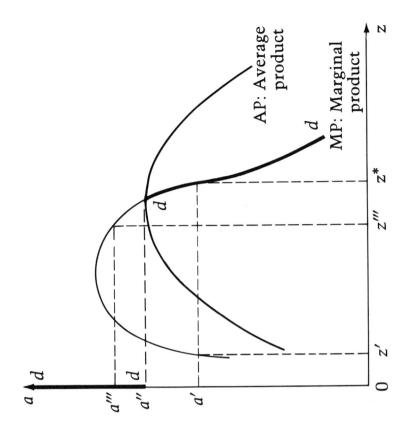
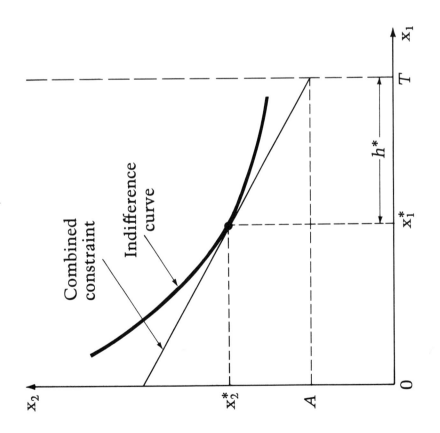

Figures 14.1, 14.2

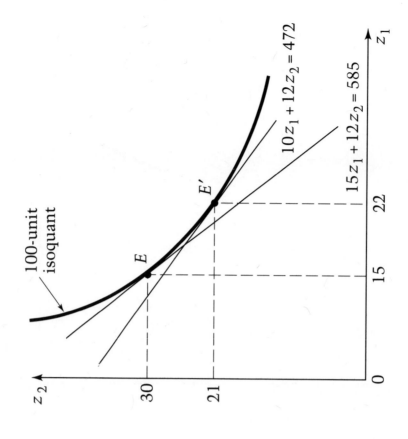

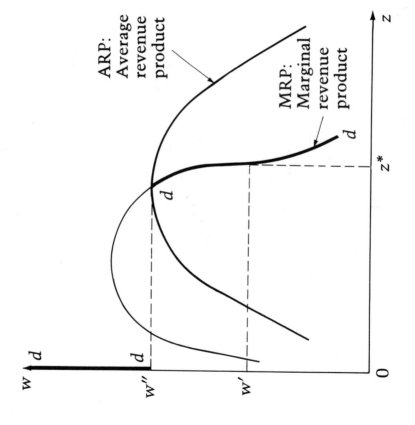

Figures 14.3, 14.4

Eaton and Eaton: MICROECONOMICS, Second Edition

© 1991, W. H. Freeman and Company

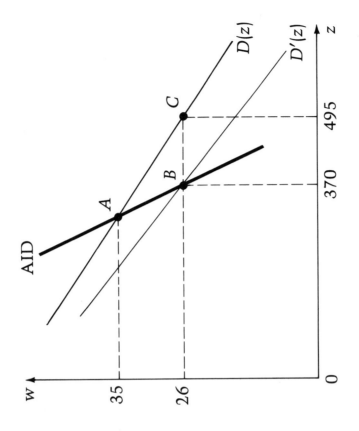
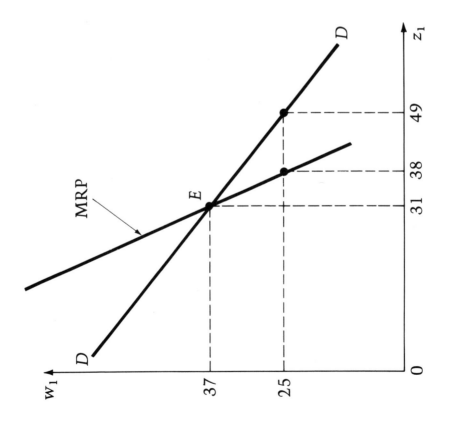

Figures 14.5, 14.6

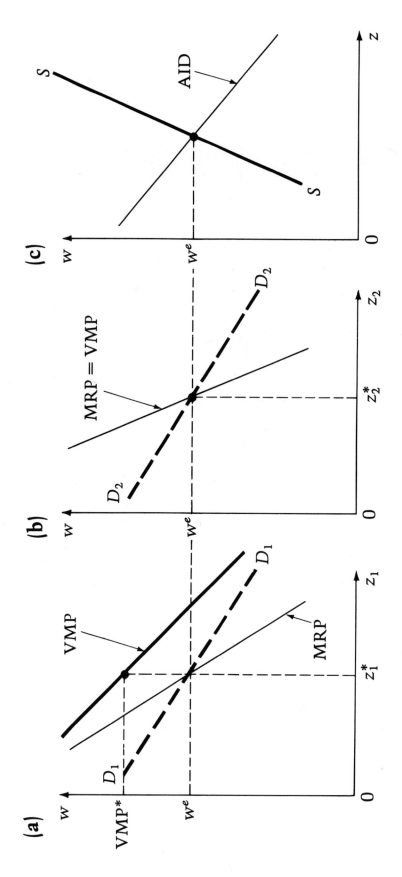

Figure 14.7

Figure 14.8

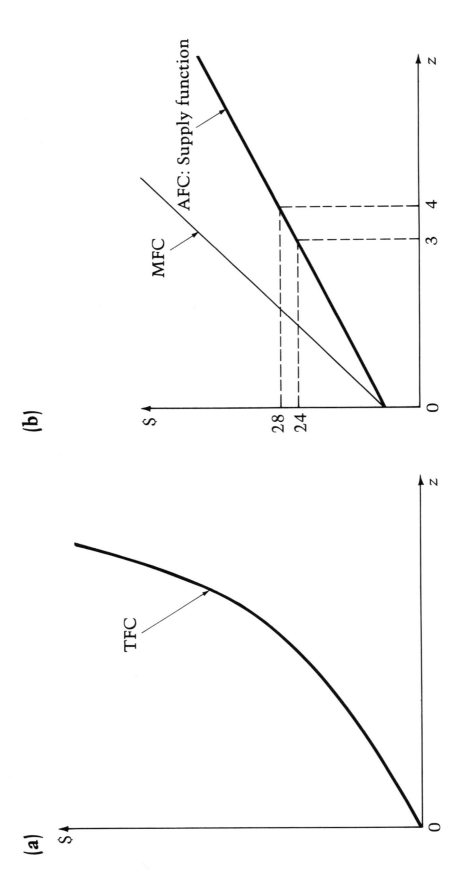

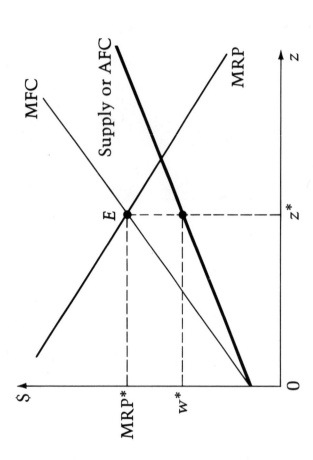

Figures 14.9, 14.10

Eaton and Eaton: MICROECONOMICS, Second Edition

© 1991, W. H. Freeman and Company

Pages 397, 398

Figures 14.11, 14.12

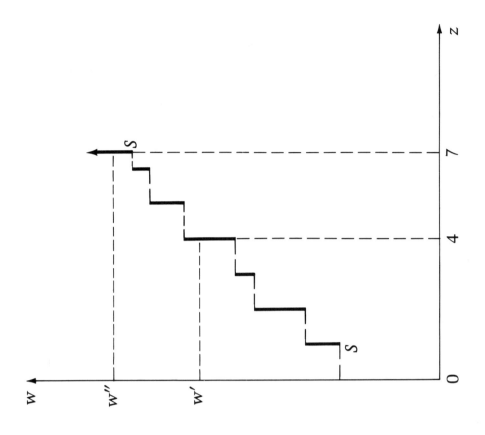
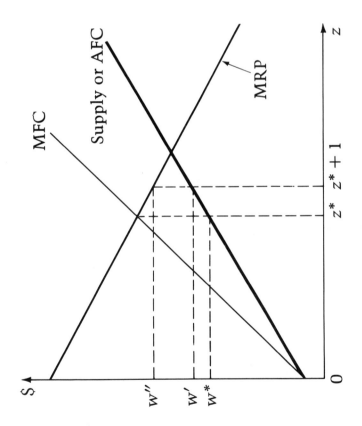

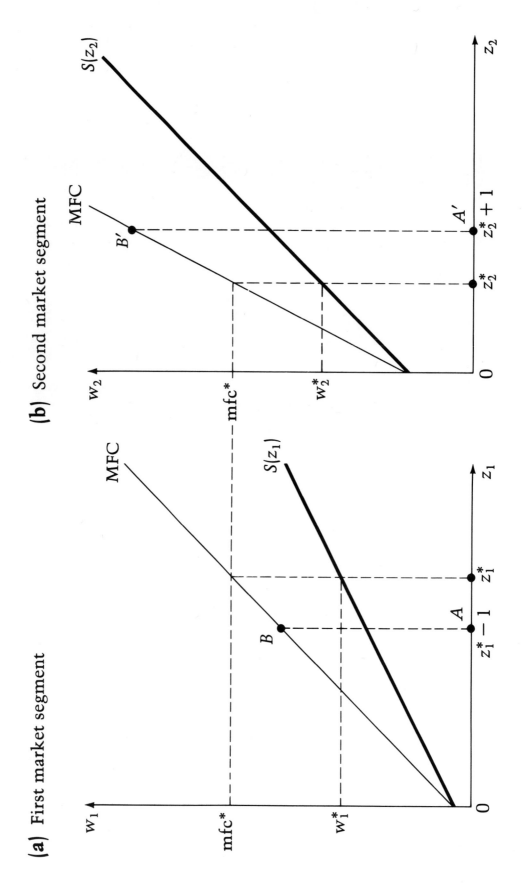

Figure 14.13

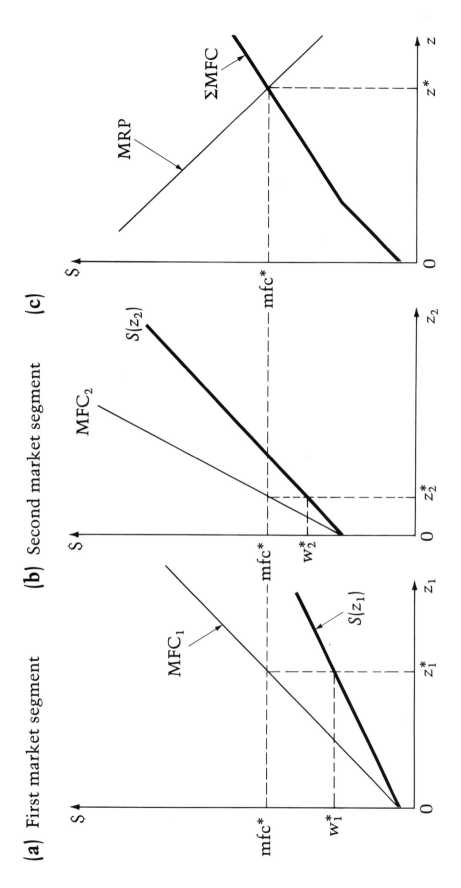

Figure 14.14

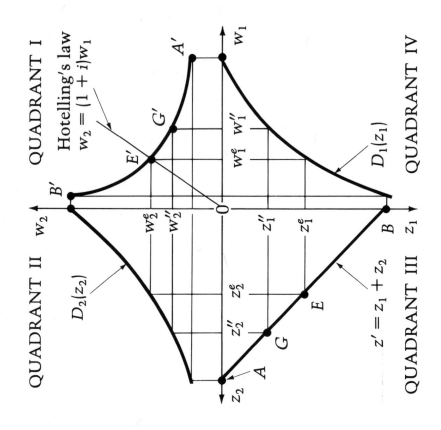

Figures 14.15, 14.16

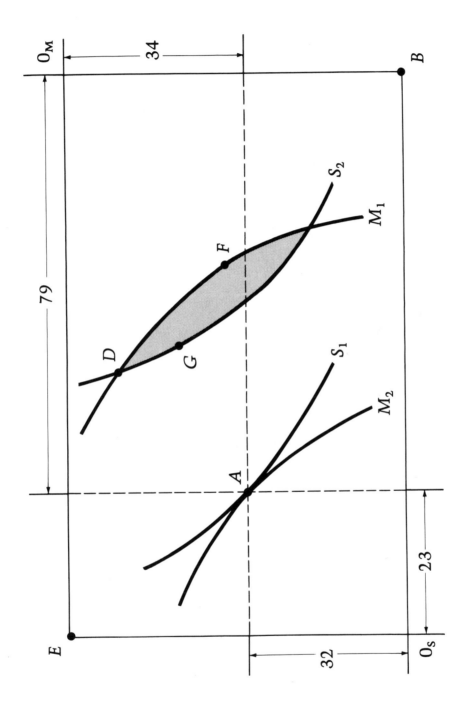

Figure 15.1

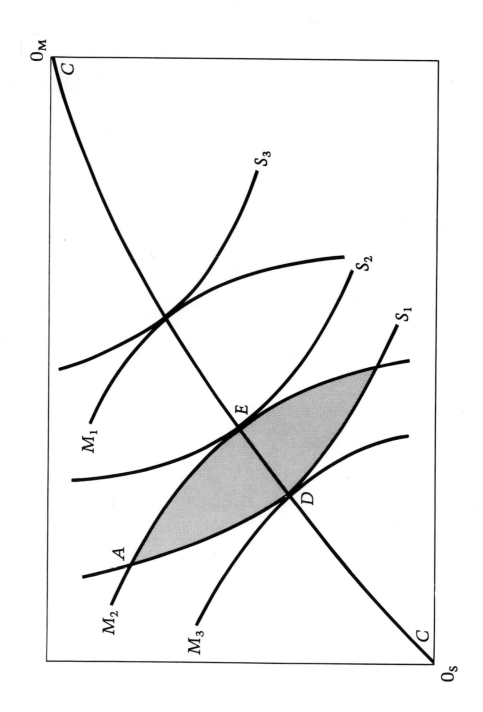

Figure 15.2

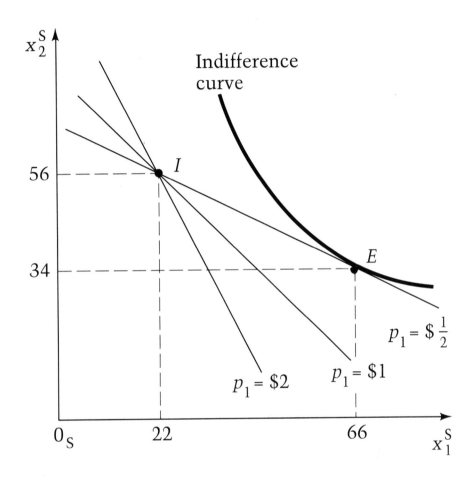

Figure 15.3

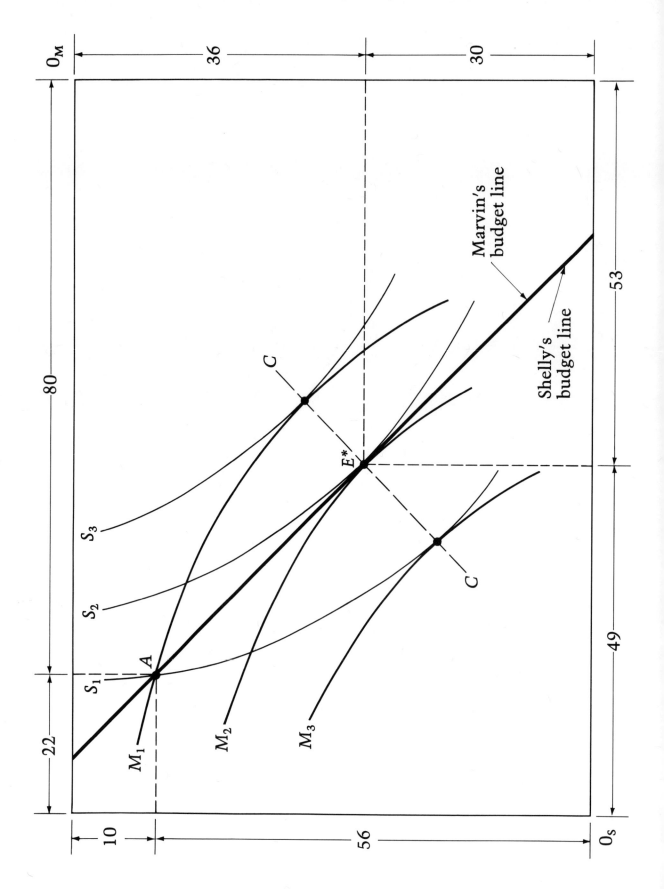

Figure 15.4

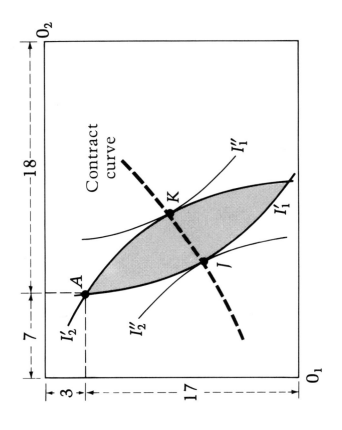
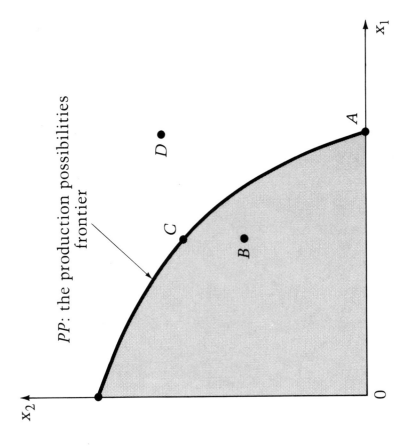

Figures 15.5, 15.6

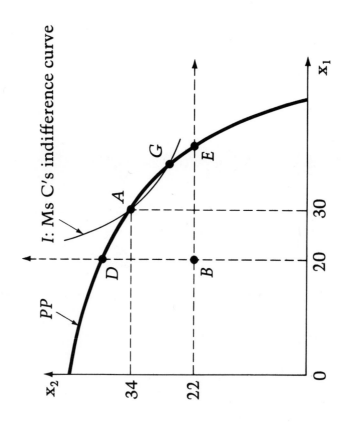

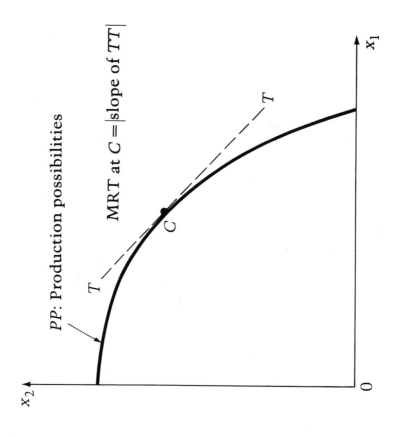

Figures 15.7, 15.8

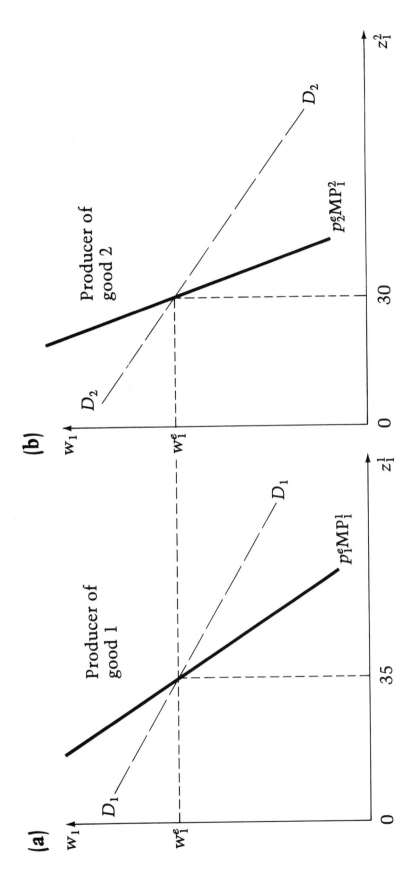

Figure 15.9

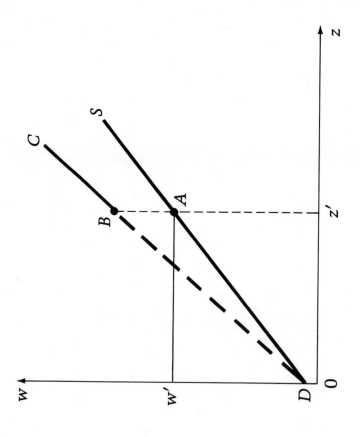

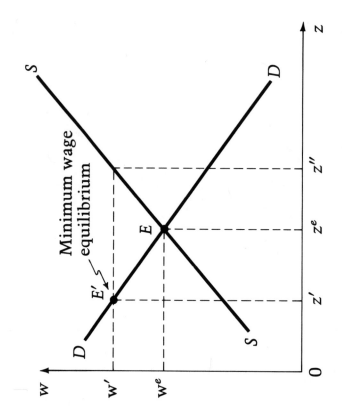

Figures 16.1, 16.2

Eaton and Eaton: MICROECONOMICS, Second Edition

© 1991, W. H. Freeman and Company

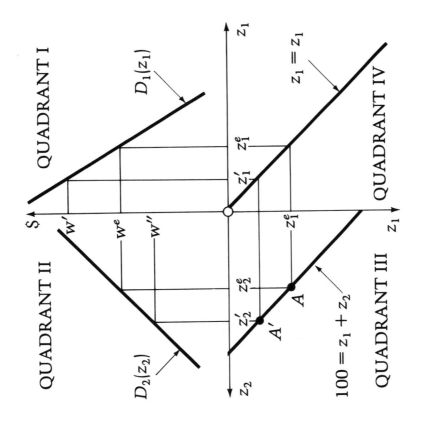

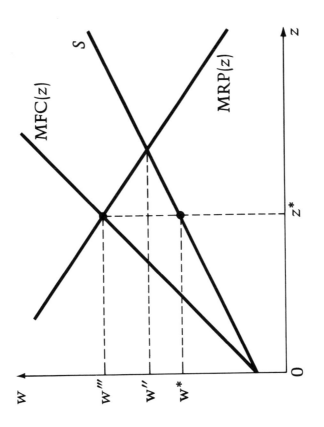

Figures 16.3, 16.4

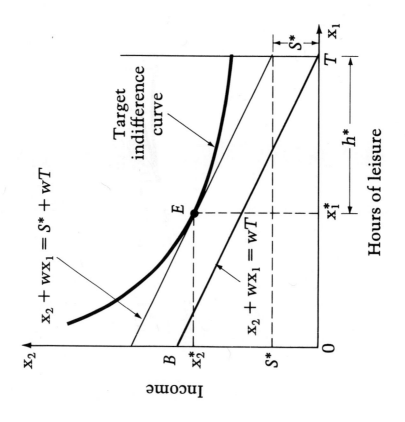

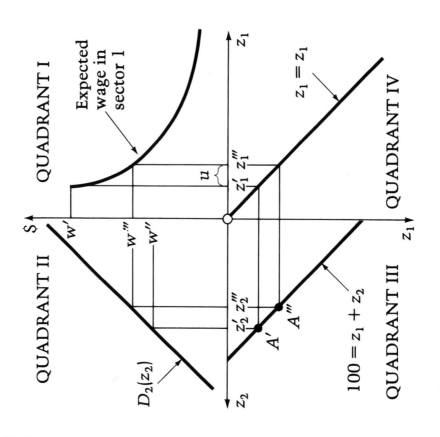

Figures 16.5, 16.6

Eaton and Eaton: MICROECONOMICS, Second Edition
© 1991, W. H. Freeman and Company

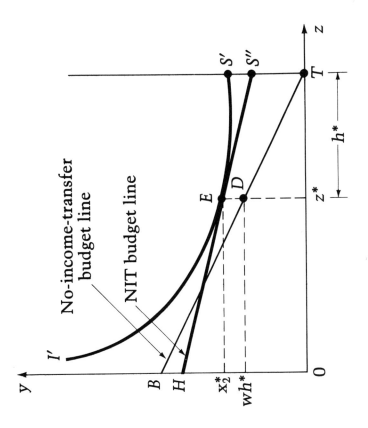

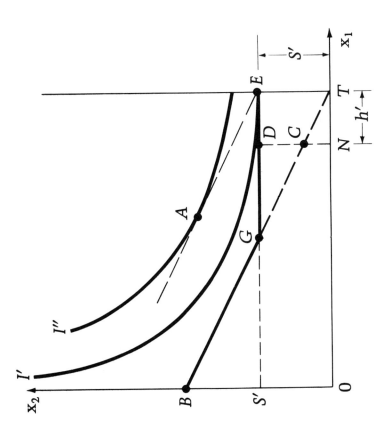

Figures 16.7, 16.8

Eaton and Eaton: MICROECONOMICS, Second Edition

© 1991, W. H. Freeman and Company

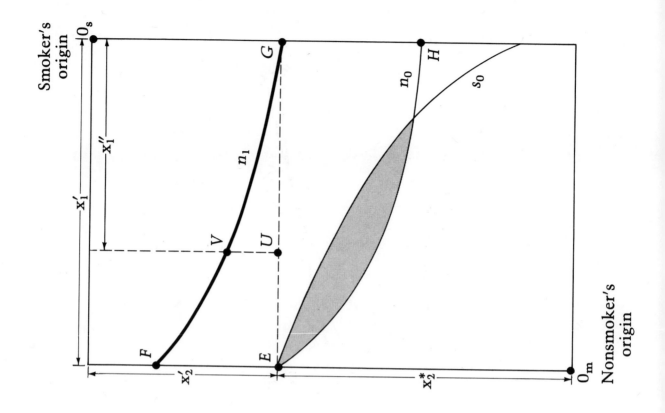

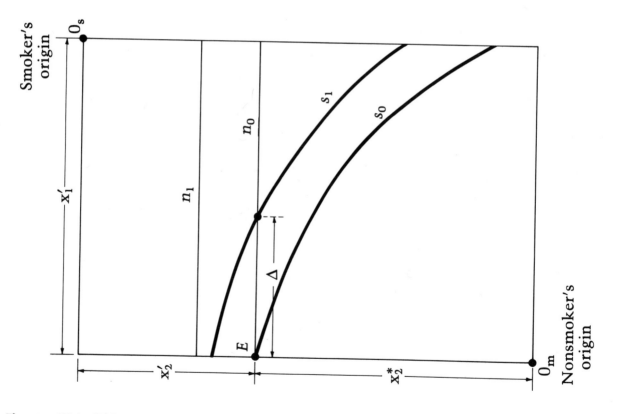

Figures 17.1, 17.2

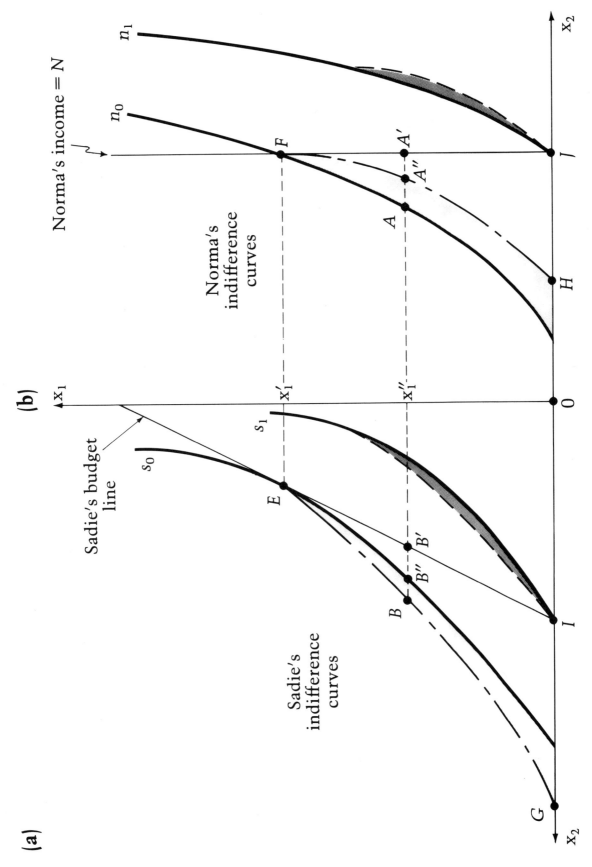

Figure 17.3

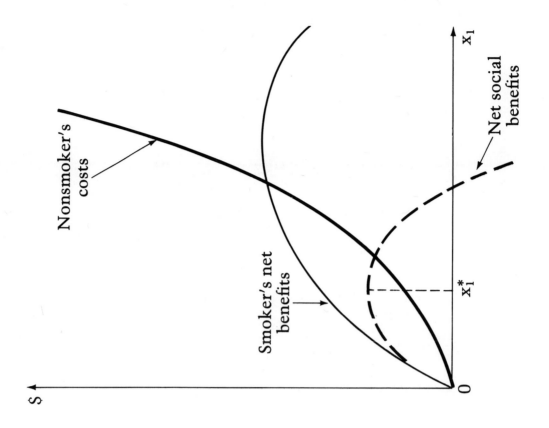
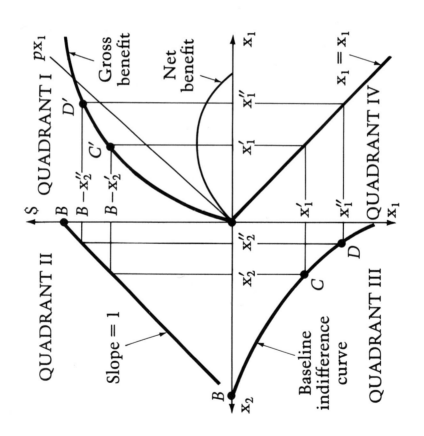

Figures 17.4, 17.5

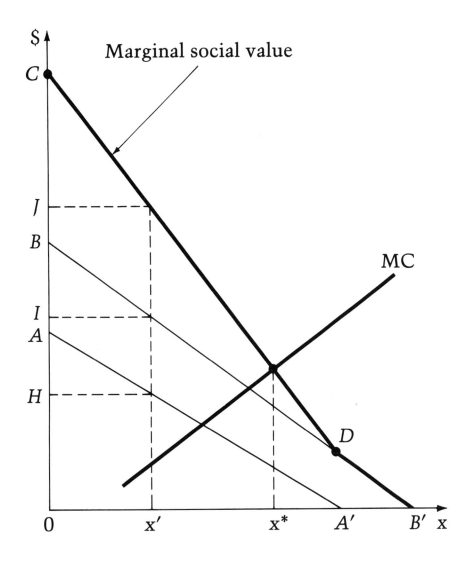

Figure 17.6

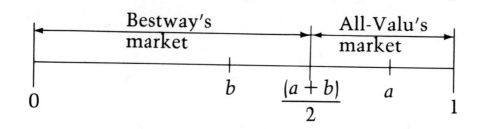

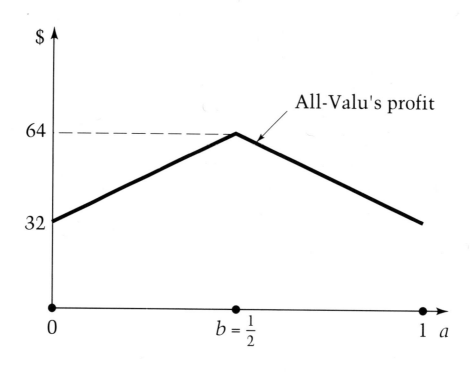

Figures A1.1, A1.2

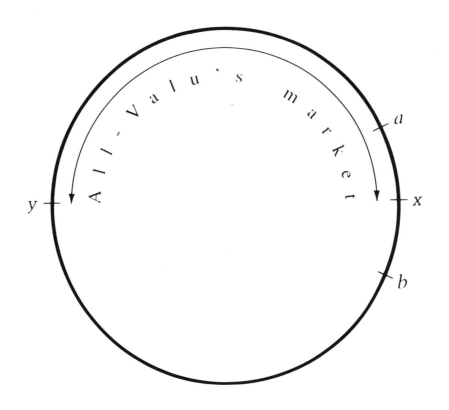

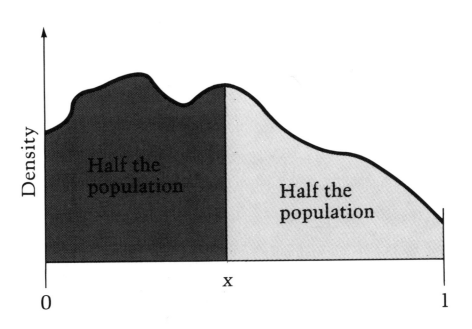

Figures A1.3, A1.4

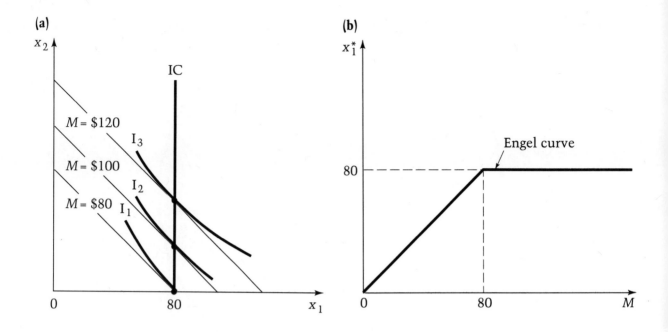
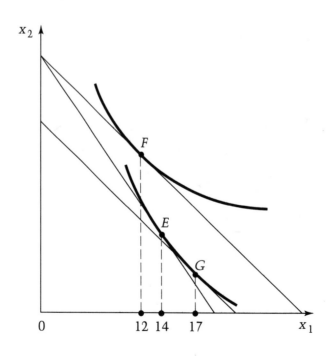

Figures A4.1, A4.2

Eaton and Eaton: MICROECONOMICS, Second Edition

© 1991, W. H. Freeman and Company

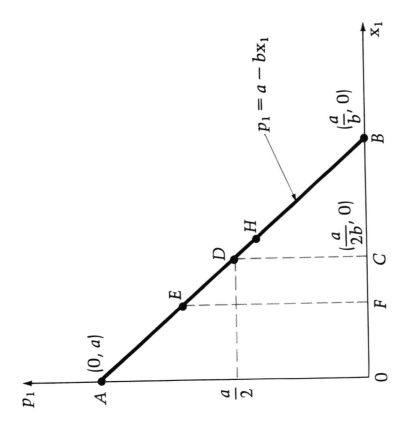

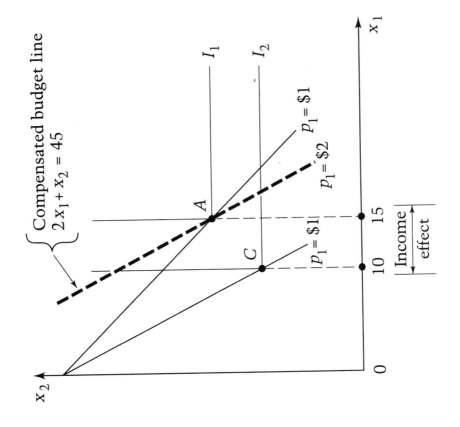

Figures A4.3, A4.4

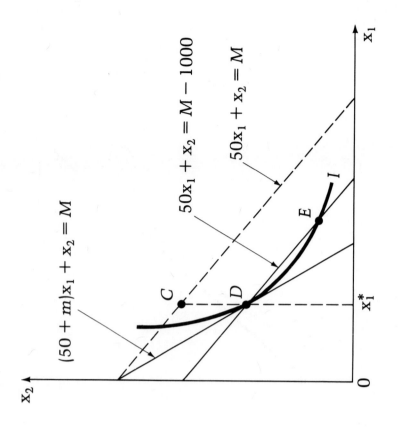

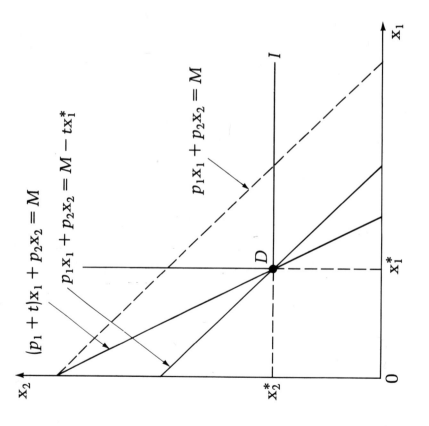

Figures A5.1, A5.2

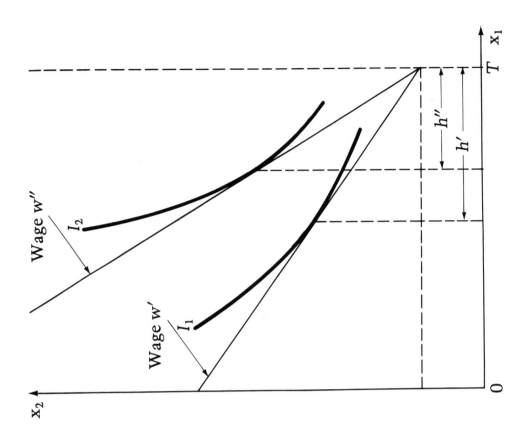
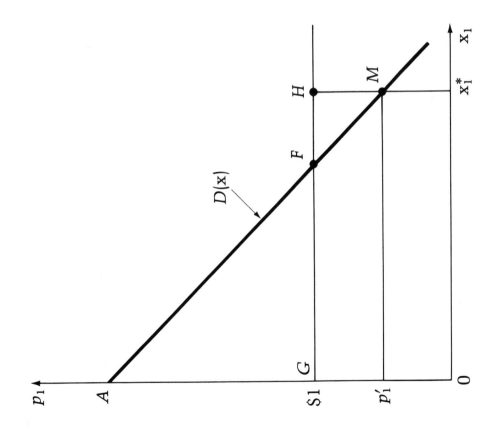

Figures A5.3, A5.4

Eaton and Eaton: MICROECONOMICS, Second Edition

© 1991, W. H. Freeman and Company

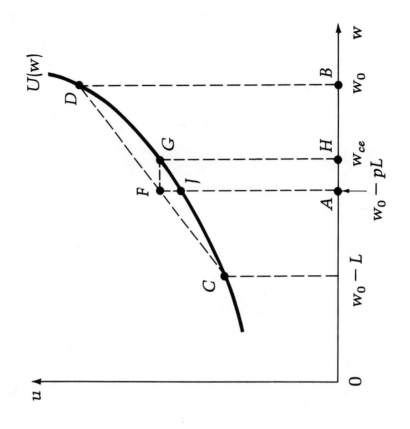
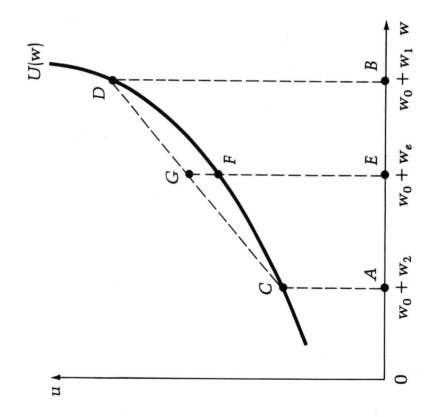

Figures A6.1, A6.2

Eaton and Eaton: MICROECONOMICS, Second Edition

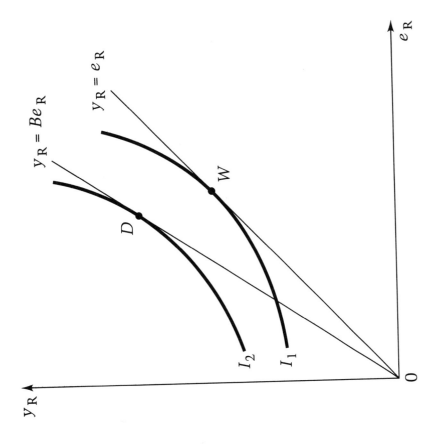

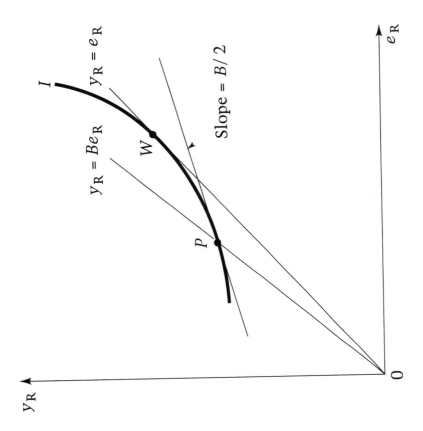

Figures A7.1, A7.2

Eaton and Eaton: MICROECONOMICS, Second Edition

© 1991, W. H. Freeman and Company

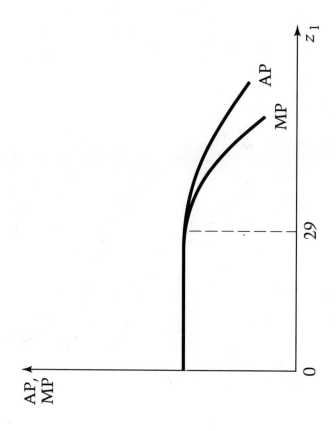

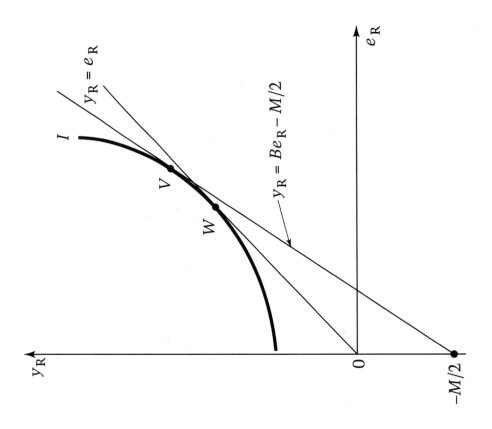

Figures A7.3, A8.1

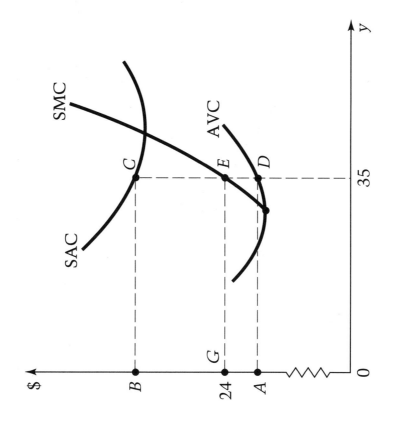
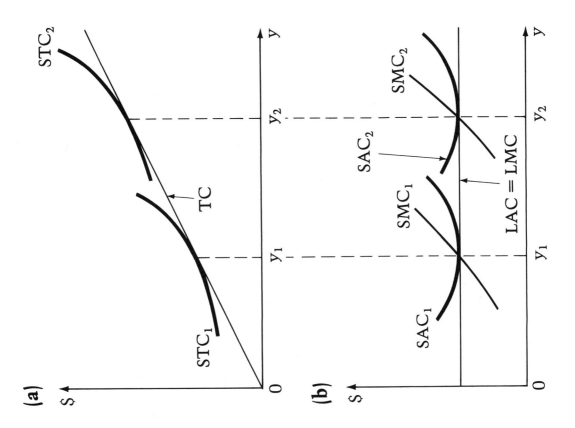

Figures A9.1, A10.1

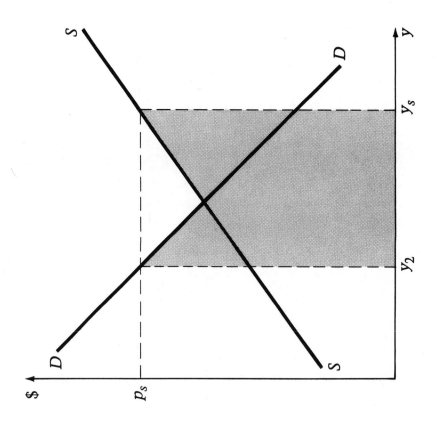

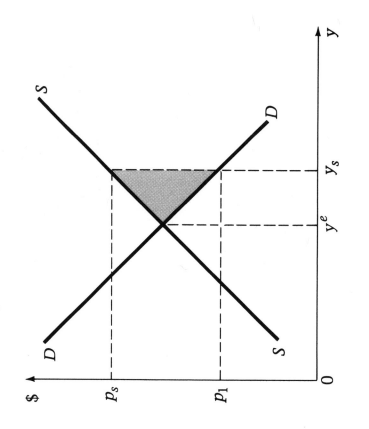

Figures A10.2, A10.3

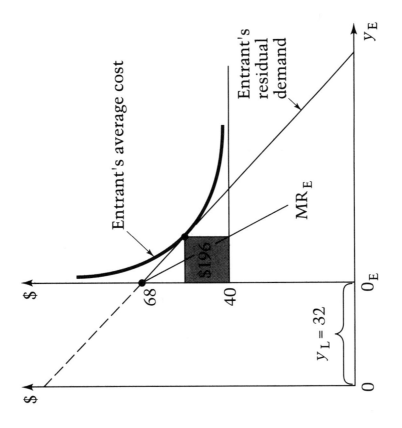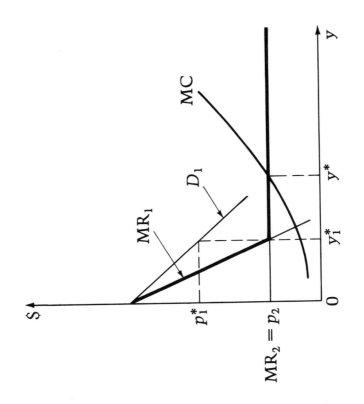

Figures A11.1, A12.1

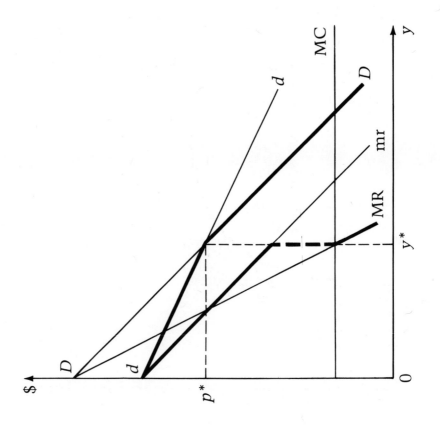
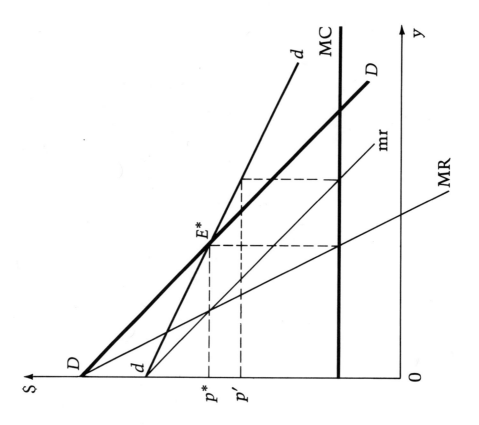

Figures A13.1, A13.2

Eaton and Eaton: MICROECONOMICS, Second Edition

© 1991, W. H. Freeman and Company

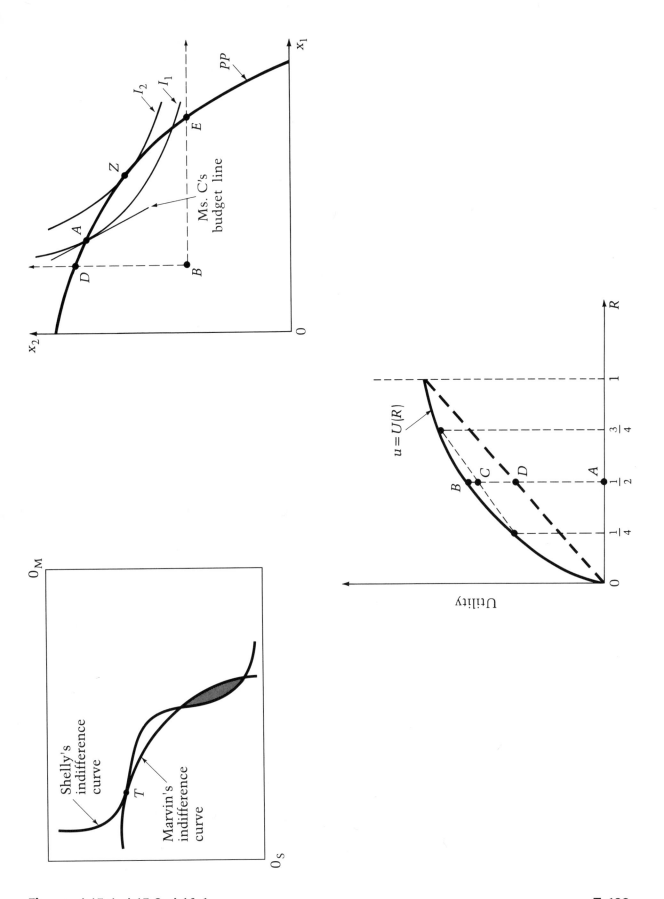

Figures A15.1, A15.2, A16.1

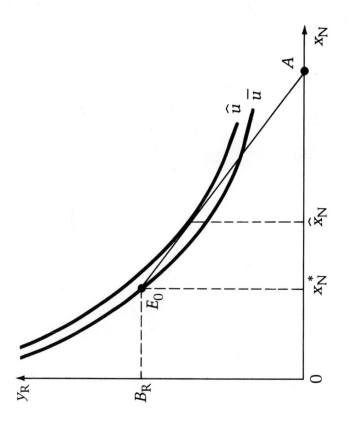
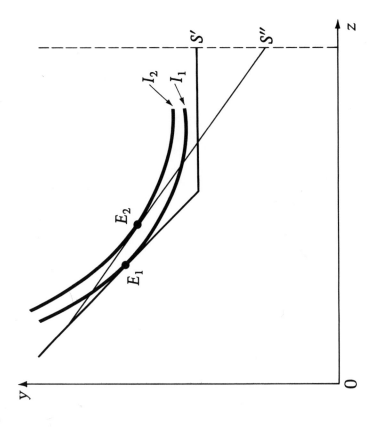

Figures A16.2, A17.1

Eaton and Eaton: MICROECONOMICS, Second Edition